THE STORY OF THE YORKVILLE HIGH SCHOOL WORLD WAR II BANNER

Gwendolyn McCaffrey McReynolds

Varnavas Press
Memphis, Tennessee
2015

Varnavas Press is a subsidiary of the Discipleship Ministry Team. It was established in order to provide a publishing outlet for Cumberland Presbyterians. However, publication by Varnavas Press does not imply the endorsement of the Discipleship Ministry Team, the Ministry Council, or the Cumberland Presbyterian Denomination. The content of Varnavas Press publications remains wholly the property and the responsibility of their respective copyright holders.

First Edition, First Printing, April 2015

ISBN-13: 978-0692306352
ISBN-10: 0692306358

DEDICATION

James Robert McCaffrey

I dedicate this book to my parents who instilled in me the love and appreciation for our men and women who serve our nation. In memory of my father, retired SMSGT James Robert McCaffrey, who served as a Seaman First Class in the Navy during World War II aboard the USS Vesuvius and then in 1950 joined the Air Force. His last duty station before retiring on 1 August 1969 was with the Joint Chiefs of Staff at the Pentagon. He is buried in the Yorkville Cemetery and is listed on the Yorkville Veterans' Memorial. In honor of my mother, Bettye Jean Loggins McCaffrey Ellis, who made a home filled with love where ever Daddy was stationed and especially when Daddy was sent overseas. In addition I wish to thank Matt Gore for being my editor and supporter during this project.

Gwen McReynolds

THE STORY OF THE YORKVILLE HIGH SCHOOL WORLD WAR II BANNER

FOREWORD

In this book, Gwendolyn McCaffrey McReynolds, Gwen to almost everyone, explores the Yorkville (Tennessee) High School World War II Service Banner and those persons commemorated or memorialized in the stitches with the enthusiasm and determination of a committed local historian and genealogist.

As a historian and a collector of militaria, I have been aware of "service flags" or "service banners" for just about as long as I can remember. The Service Flag, sometimes called the "Blue Star Flag" or the "Boys in Service Flag," originated in World War I. Captain Robert L. Queisser, 5th Ohio Infantry, designed the original service flag to honor his two sons serving in France. The image captured the public imagination and became the unofficial symbol of a child in service.[1]

In 1918, President Woodrow Wilson approved a Women's Committee of the Council of National Defenses suggestion that mothers who had lost a child to the war wear a gold star on their traditional black mourning arm band. Eventually, gold stars came to be used on service flags to indicate the death of the service member.[2]

During World War II Americans enthusiastically resumed the display of service flags.[3] Many flags were hand crafted but some were manufactured and the image also appeared on a variety of commercially available products, like decals. Besides individual flags it became a common practice to make a flag representing the "boys in service" from an entire organization or community. This was probably most often done by churches but was certainly not limited to communities of faith.

My own first experience with this uniquely American iconography came, I believe, on a trip to Mac's Surplus in Aberdeen, South Dakota, worlds away from Yorkville, Tennessee. It would have been in 1968 or 1969 and my fascination with all things military was only just beginning. At the time, Mac's was a treasure trove of military surplus.

On this particular visit, I was fascinated by a bin full of waterslide decals in glassine envelopes. Each decal bore a single blue star on a white field with a red border. I had no idea what they were but they cost 5¢ each, in my mind they were military, and they were really cool. Neither the clerk nor my Dad had any idea what they were, the image having fallen somewhat out of vogue by the Vietnam era. Still, I recall that I invested my quarter in five of them.

It did not take long to encounter someone who was familiar with exactly what that symbol represented. Somewhere in one of my family's many moves, the decals were lost, but I never forgot their special symbolism.

Matthew H. Gore
April 21, 2015

---

[1] "Blue Star Mothers Service Flag," Last modified 2008, accessed April 21, 2015, http://www.bluestarmothers.org/service-flag.

[2] *Ibid.*

[3] *Ibid.*

THE STORY OF THE YORKVILLE HIGH SCHOOL WWII BANNER

Alline Taylor, who was the Home Economics teacher at Yorkville High School, and her students created the World War II Service Flag with its 118 blue stars to hang in the halls of the Yorkville School so that all who were attending the school and those who entered the halls could keep in mind the young men and women who had attended the school at sometime during their childhood and were "now" serving during World War II. Only 46 of the boys listed graduated from Yorkville High School.

VIEW OF SCHOOL BUILDING

 Many of the young men entered the service with a grammar school or less than 4 years of high school or moved out of the community and graduated elsewhere. Mrs. Alline and her students created the flag between the 1942-1944 school years.

The original Service Flag was machine sewn. With each star hand embroidered and then appliquéd by machine. The thirty seven stars nearest the YHS initials were hand sewn on as more young men and one young woman joined the military service. Gold stars were added to cover the blue stars of Roy Fay Edmiston, Harry Wilson Jones, and Wilson Ray Scott when these young men died in the service of their country.

When the banner was taken down from the high school walls a number of years after the war, it was given to Gabe and Hortense Jones, parents of Wilson Jones. After their deaths, the flag was in the possession of Congressman Ed Jones, brother of Wilson and oldest son of Gabe and Hortense. Bettye Loggins McCaffrey, secretary to Congressman Jones and sister of Reuben and Phillip Loggins, whose stars are on the flag, became the keeper of the banner for Congressman Jones. After the death of Congressman Jones, the banner was returned to public display in the Yorkville City Hall. Today the banner hangs in the Yorkville Community Center. The flag was framed with archival materials in 2014 and was dedicated during a reunion of former Yorkville students on May 2, 2014. Only one of the men, Jack Ramsey, was able to attend the 2014 dedication. Most of the men listed had passed away.

THE "BOYS" AND ONE "GIRL"

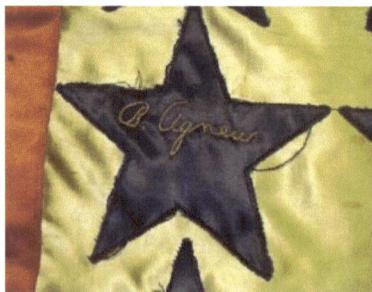

Agnew, B. [1]- *possibly* Robert M. Agnew, 25 June 1910-29 Jan 1992. He was married to Mary Frances Lumpkin in the 1940 Rutherford, Gibson County Census and is buried in the Rutherford Cemetery. He was the son of William J. and Nellie Cook Agnew. William was a railroad agent. [His brother, Jack T. Agnew served as a TEC 4 US Army WWII according to his U.S. Veterans Gravesite information 27 Jun 1912-12 April 2003]

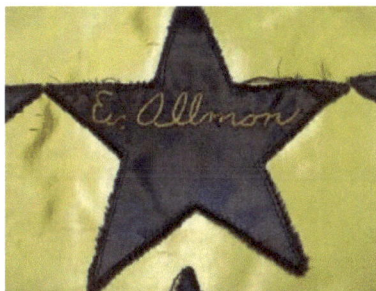

Allmon, E. [2] .- Everett Allmon: 13 June 1915-10 Sept 2002 ; Buried Chapel Hill Memorial Garden, Lansing, MI; son of Bennie Elmer and Annie Baldridge Allmon who married 9 Sept 1910 in Dyer County; 1930 District 8 Gibson County Census lists Everett, age 14, living with his parents. Military inscription: CPL US Marine Corps [Brother Thomas Ewing "Earl "Allmon served also]

Listed as Everett Allmon (1915) on Fold3: http://www.fold3.com

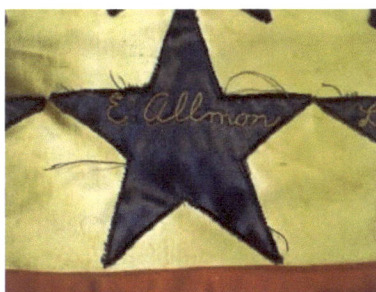

Allmon, E. [12] Thomas Ewing "Earl" Allmon; 15 Feb 1922-6 Oct 1987; son of Bennie Elmer and Annie Baldridge Allmon and husband of Maidell Collins whom he married 17 August 1943 in St. Louis. (She was from Obion County.); 1930 District 8 Gibson Co census lists Earl, age 8, living with his parents: 1940 Census shows Seaman in Naval Operating Base, Norfolk, VA ; Military Marker: Machinist 's Mate 1c USN, Wounded in Action ;Served on USS Barnett, USS Twiggs (DD-127), USS MCawley; Enlisted 17 Feb 1940 in the Navy

Muster Rolls: search for Thomas Ewing Allmon on Fold3: http://www.fold3.com

Austin, K. [5]-*Cannot locate*

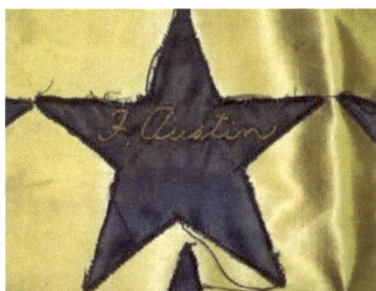

Austin, F. [8] Farris Austin **CLASS OF 1937**; 1 May 1919-28 March 2001 Union City [Find A Grave Memorial# 41378984]; son of R. C. and Vivian Smith Austin who marred 24 August 1918 in Dyer county; 1930 District 6 Dyer County Census lists Farris L. Austin, age 10, with his parents: enlisted in Army on 28 January 1943 from Dyer County with 1 year college; ***Listed on the Veteran's Memorial** Listed as Farris L Austin on www.fold3.com

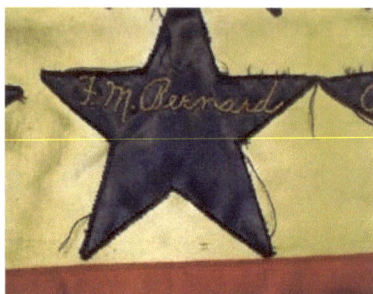

Barnard, F. M. [4] .-Freddie M. Barnard, born 1922, son of Fred and Allie Reynolds Barnard (note: Maiden name is from her signature on her husband's death certificate); 1930 District 8, Gibson County census lists F.M, age 7, living with his parents. Enlisted 12 Oct 1942 in Army in Weakley County with 1 year High School.

Listed as Freddie M. Barnard www.fold3.com

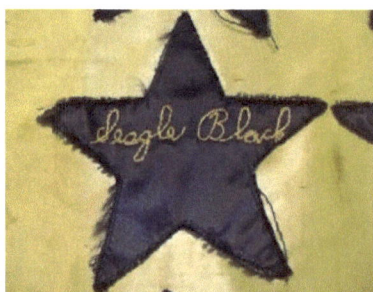

Black, Seagle [10] -Edwin Seagle Black-10 Oct 1924-12 Feb 2010; buried Bobbitt Cemetery in Dyer [Find A Grave Memorial# 127975473] son of Osie Leck and Fannie Lee Coleman Black who married 4 July 1908 in Gibson County; [brother William Black served also] Enlisted Army Air Corps on 16 January 1945 and was discharged 16 February 1947 according to his discharge papers.

*Listed on the Veteran's Memorial

Seagle's daughter Charlotte said, " Daddy was ready to ship out when the war ended. Mom was expecting me at the time."

31 July 1946 TRI-CITY REPORTER: "Pfc Seagle Black of Vancouver, Wash....has enlisted for one year to serve the U.S.A. He is a memograph operator in the personnel office in Vancouver."

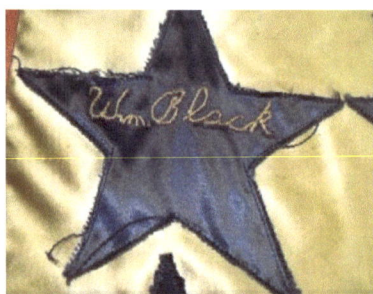

Black, William [1] -, William Wilson Black-20 Sept 1915-7 Feb 1990, buried in Rutherford Cemetery [Findagrave # 16677502], PFC U.S. Army, Enlisted 9 Aug 1941 with 3 years High School; son of Osie Leck and Fannie Lee Coleman Black. [Brothers: Seagle and William] ***Listed on the Veteran's Memorial**

Listed as William W. Black (His is the 1915 Tennessee one.) on Fold3: http://www.fold3.com

Interesting fact: Most of the Yorkville boys who fought in World War II had grown up without electricity in their homes. Electricity did not come to Yorkville until 1938.

Boucher, L. [1] James Lemuel Boucher, 8 Jan 1914-22 March 1999; buried Yorkville [# Find A Grave Memorial# 127511382]son of Earl Daniel and Demmie Earl Holland Boucher who married 21 July 1912 in Gibson County ; Enlisted in the Army with 4 years High school on 9 Jul 1941 and served until 4 Oct 1945 Rank: TEC 5 ***Listed on the Veteran's Memorial**

Listed as James L. Boucher (His birth 1914 Tennessee on Fold3: http://www.fold3.com

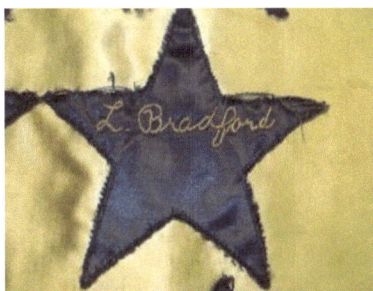

Bradford, L. [5] Leon Harrison Bradford,: Born 8 Oct 1924-29 Sept 1991.,buried at Yorkville [Find A Grave Memorial# 26782202]; In the Rural Gibson County 1940 Census he is noted as nephew living with Thomas and Louella Scott; enlisted 27 Sept 1944 in Army with 2 years High School. Sgt. US Army ***Listed on the Veteran's Memorial**

Listed as Leon Bradford (1924) on Fold3: http://www.fold3.com

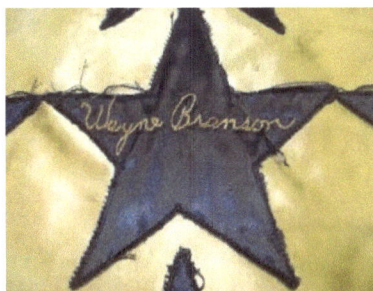

Branson, Wayne [13] Harold Wayne Branson; **CLASS OF 1934** 19 May 1916-5 March 1989 in Lake Co, Florida; son of Clarence E. and Willie Jetton Branson who married 1 May 1907 in Gibson County; Served in the US Navy aboard USS Salamonie (AD -26), USS Capitaine (SS-336), USS Gurnard (SS-254); Enlisted 9 April 1941 in Nashville ***Listed on the Veteran's Memorial**
 Muster Rolls listed on Fold3.com.

Military picture from Art_Kendall of La Conner, Washington from Wayne Branson's Ancestry.com

Brown, J. T. [4] Joseph Thomas Brown; son of Robert O and Orilla Terrill Brown who married 19 January 1919 in Gibson County, Tennessee; 1930 Granite City, Madison, Illinois Census lists Robert O Brown, 32; Orilla Brown, 32; Verlon E., 10; Joseph T, 6; Delbert H., 2 5/12; 1935 Inferred and 1940 Rural, Gibson County Census lists Joseph 16; Delbert, 12; Deloris, 8

According to J.T.'s brother, J.T. was a Marine who served in the Pacific Theatre during World War II. One of his duty stations was the Philippines.

Brown, Verlon [3] CLASS OF 1938, PRESIDENT/picture Verlon E.. Brown; 14 Feb 1920- 2 December 1999 and buried in Clinton Cemetery, Clinton, North Carolina; son of Robert O and Orilla Terrill Brown who married 19 January 1919 in Gibson County, Tennessee; 1930 Granite City, Madison, Illinois Census lists Robert O Brown, 32; Orilla Brown, 32; Verlon E., 10; Joseph T, 6; Delbert H., 2 5/12; Enlisted 4 Sept 1940 in Marines; 30 Sept 1940 private at First Recruit Battalion, Recruit Depot Marine Barracks, Parris Island, SC1 :; April 1941 USS Texas as private in Marine Detachment; October 1942 Mess Company, School Bn, Tc, Camp Lejeune, New River, NC serving as a Mess Sergeant; Oct 1943 now a Staff Sergeant at Camp Lejeune; April 1944 now a Tech Sergeant at Camp Lejeune; April 1945 Barracks Detachment, Marine Barracks, Norfolk Navy Yard, Portsmouth, Virginia

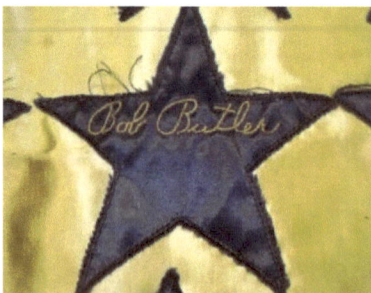

Butler, Bob [12] Robert C. Butler, born 1924; son of Chester and Lillie Butler ; 1930 District 8 Gibson County Census lists Bobby Butler, age 6, living with his parents. enlisted 26 May 1943 in Army with 3 years High School

Listed as Robert C Butler on Fold3: http://www.fold3.com

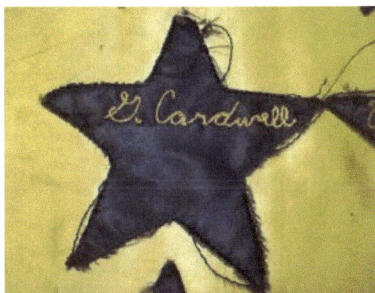

Cardwell, G. [10] George W. Cardwell, 28 April 1925-9 October 2003 Stark Co., Ohio. son of J. Walter and Queen Boucher Cardwell who married 1921 in Gibson County. 1930 Gibson County Census lists James C, age 7, and George W, age 4, living with their parents. ; Enlisted 16 October 1945 in the Army with 4 years High School [George and J.C. Cardwell are brothers.]

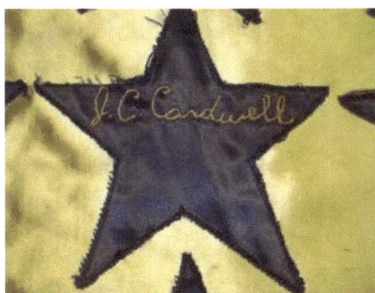

Cardwell, J.C. [2] James Calvin Leonard Cardwell; 23 Sep 1922 - 7 Jun 1993 San Joaquin Valley National Cemetery [Find A Grave Memorial# 463198], son of J. Walter and Queen Boucher Cardwell who married 1921 in Gibson County; 1930 District 8 Gibson County Census lists James C, age 7, and George W, age 4, living with their parents. Military Service: 5 November 1940, BM2 US Navy on military marker, served aboard USS Wasp (CV-18) ,USS Whicita (CA-45) , USS Windham Bay (CVE-92) USS Chevalier (DD-805) [note: service #295 81 34)], George and J.C. Cardwell, brothers]

Muster Rolls on Fold3.com under James C I Cardwell [Ancestry.com also and easier to locate!)

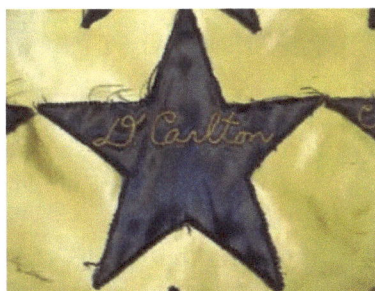

Carlton, D. [13] Dennis Wayne Carlton; 1 Nov 1918 in the Nebo Community -28 June 2007 in the Veteran's Home in Humboldt; buried in Yorkville [Find A Grave Memorial# 113396432]; son of William

Henry and Grace Pace Carlton who married 15 September 1912 in Gibson County. ; 1930 District 8 Gibson County Census lists Wayne, age 11, living with his parents.; Enlisted 29 Oct 1941 in U.S. Navy; Navy Muster roll for 31 December 1941 Section Base: "Nav. Tra. Sta. NOB, Norfolk, Va. for Instruction in Armed Guard School"
*Listed on the Veteran's Memorial

Ron Carlton gives this information about his uncle: "he was on a Merchant ship during the war, and I think he was in several foreign ports during the war" Ron also provided the picture.

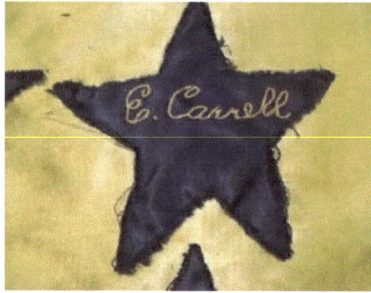

Carrell, E [6] Everett Edward Carrell, **Member of the 1944 YHS Basket Ball Team.** (*see page 49*) 30 Sept 1927-Oct 1976]He was living in Somerville Tennessee when he died in a plane crash; son of Lonnie and Lena Davis Carrell; 1930 District 8 Gibson County Census lists Lonnie, age 6, and Everett E, age 2 6/12, living with their parents. ; 1940 Rural Gibson County Census lists: Lonnie B Carrell (48), Lenna Carrell (45), Everett Carrell (12), Lonnie Carrell (13), Juanita Carrell (13); Enlisted 10 January 1946 in US Army with 4 years High School; [Brothers: Everett and Lonnie both enlisted]

Carrell, L. [5]-Lonnie Carrell ; 6 Jan 1924-24 July 1986; buried Yorkville [Find A Grave Memorial# 113441717] Enlisted 14 August 1945 in Navy ; son of Lonnie and Lena Davis Carrell who married 31 December 1910 in Gibson County; 1930 District 8 Gibson County Census lists Lonnie, age 6, and Everett E, age 2 6/12, living with their parents. ; 1940 Rural Gibson County Census lists: Lonnie B Carrell (48), Lenna Carrell (45), Everett Carrell (12), Lonnie Carrell (13), Juanita Carrell (13**) *Listed on the Veteran's Memorial** [Brothers: Everett and Lonnie both enlisted]

Memorial page on Fold3.com listed as Lonnie Carrell provides enlistment information and death dates
During the Yorkville School Reunion on 4 May 2014, a cousin of both boys shared that there was a period of "creative spelling" in school for Lonnie, but the legal spelling for his name is Carrell.

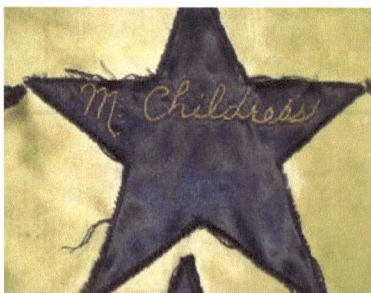

Childress, M. [3] William Malcolm Childress; 27 March 1923-1 Feb 2006 Doniphan, Missouri; son of Claude and Lena Marie Neil Childress who married 19 July 1918 in Gibson County ; 1930 District 8, Gibson County, TN Census lists Malcom, age 7 with his parents. ; According to U.S. World War II Army Enlistment Records, 1938-1946 he enlisted in Army 25 January 1943 from Gibson County.

Clark, Robert [14] Robert M. "Turtle:" Clark; son of Clayton and Annie Dee Haliburton Clark who married 3 Dec 1916 in Gibson County; 1920 District 9, Dyer County lists Robert Marton [sic], age 1, with parents Clayton and Annie D. Clark.; 1930 District 8 Gibson County Census lists Robert, age 11, with his parents. Enlisted 14 May 1941 in the Army with 4 years high school.

Sergt. Robt. M. Clark
Newbern, Tenn.

Listed as Robert M Clark on Fold3.com from Dyer County
The newspaper military picture is from the vintage scrap book of Bettye Loggins that she had received from a fellow classmate of hers, Ann Pope, for Christmas in 1943.

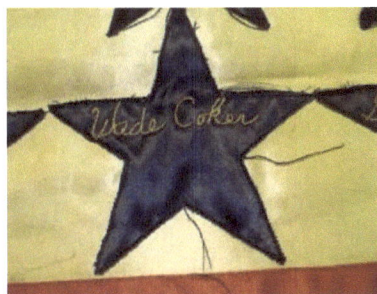

Coker, Wade [12] Willis Wade Coker; born 23 May 1919; son of George Alexander and Bertha May Sewell who were married 8 Jan 1909 in Gibson county; 1920 District 19, Gibson County Census lists Willis Wade Coker, age 7/12, with his parents; 1930 Rutherford, Gibson County Census lists Willis W., age 10, with his parents; 1940 Dyer, Gibson County Census lists Wade, age 22, with his parents and his occupation as truck driver; Information given on Briscoe, Montgomery County, North Carolina young men's draft registration: listed as Willis W. Coker, age 21, May 23, 1919, born in Rutherford, Tennessee, father is George Coker [note: His brother, Waymond Travis Coker, 16 Sept 1926 who gives his birth place as Newbern, Tenn. also has a WWII Briscoe, Montgomery Co., NC draft card. Travis lists his mother, Bertha. He and Wade are both working for Aileen Mills Co in Briscoe.]

Vintage Postcard sent to Mrs. R.W. Loggins from her son, Wison, [Reuben Wilson Loggins, Jr.] on 4 October 1941 from Columbia, South Carolina. The card is from the vintage Scrap book of his sister, Bettye.

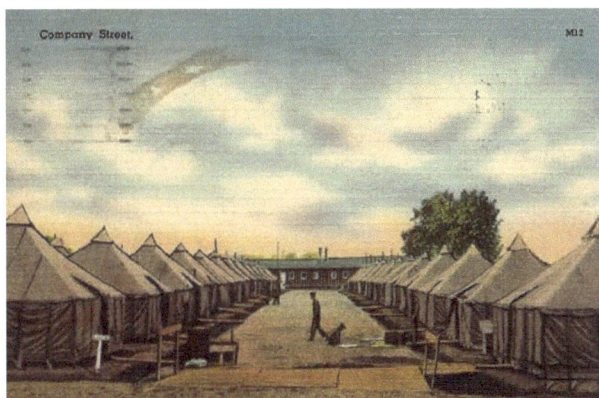

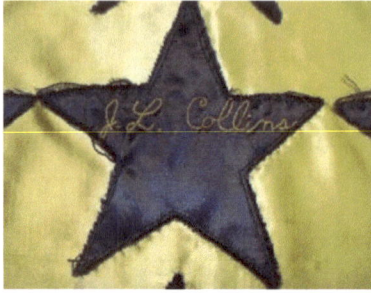

Collins, J.L. [3]-James L. "Jim" "Blackie" Collins; 24 Jan 1926-5 Jun 2001 Hernando, Mississippi, buried West Tennessee State Veterans Cemetery [Find a grave #17242452]; son of Frank A. and Mattie Harrison Collins who moved to Missouri. The 1930 and 1940 Census records list him with his parents in Pemiscot, Missouri, but he had a wealth of Collins and Harrison relatives in Gibson County with whom he lived with while he went to school at Yorkville. He was the grandson of John Boston and Amanda Barnett Collins and also James Thomas and Minnie Yarrington Harrison. He was a cousin of Nerine Collins. He played basketball for YHS where he was known as Blackie Collins.

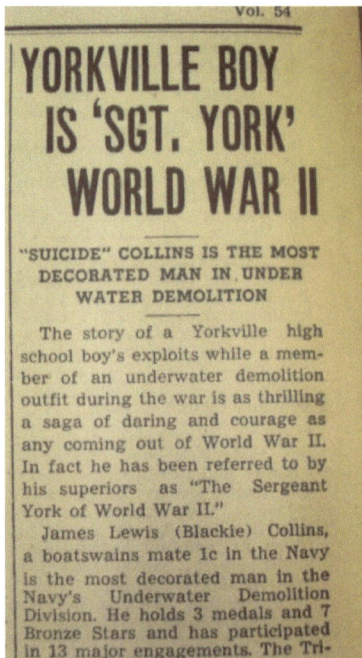

A front page article in the 10 January 1946 Tri City Reporter is headed: **YORKVILLE BOY IS 'SGT. YORK' WORLD WAR II "SUICIDE" COLLINS IS THE MOST DECORATED MAN IN UNDER WATER DEMOLITION.** (The paper's editor included a little background before including the Vice Admiral's letter) *The story of a Yorkville high school boy's exploits while a member of an underwater demolition outfit during the war is as thrilling a saga of daring and courage as any coming out of World War II. In fact he has been referred to by his superiors as "The Sergeant York of World War II."*

James Lewis (Blackie) Collins, a boatswains mate 1c in the Navy is the most decorated man in the Navy's Underwater Demolition Division. He holds 3 medals and 7 Bronze Stars and has participated in 13 major engagements. The Tri-City Reporter has received a letter from his commanding officer, Vice Admiral Brett Sheen, setting forth his exploits.

Young Collins is a grandson of Mr. and Mrs. J. T. Harrison of the Hopewell Community. His parents, Mr. and Mrs. Frank Collins, former residents of near Dyer, now live in Steele Mo.

*Of him Admiral Sheen writes: Gentlemen: I had planned, when I left the West Coast, to visit your offices in person, but circumstances beyond my control prevented my doing such. I wish you to run an article on a very praise worthy young man formerly from Yorkville. He was in my special staff and he was outstanding in every event. He was in the first **Underwater Demolition team** ever to land on enemy shores and he has been with the outfit ever since.*

He is undoubtedly the most decorated man in U.D. and why shouldn't he be? He has done more for the cause than any other man. He is a veteran of 13 major invasions. They are Saipan, Guam, Tinnian, Pelelieu, Anguar, Nzesebus, Leyte, Mondoro, Daveo, Luzon, Normandy, Okinawa, Iwo Jima.

He is the most popular man in the entire outfit. After every operation, in fact all the time, he has every one bursting their sides with his jokes and the songs he sings. He has been awarded:

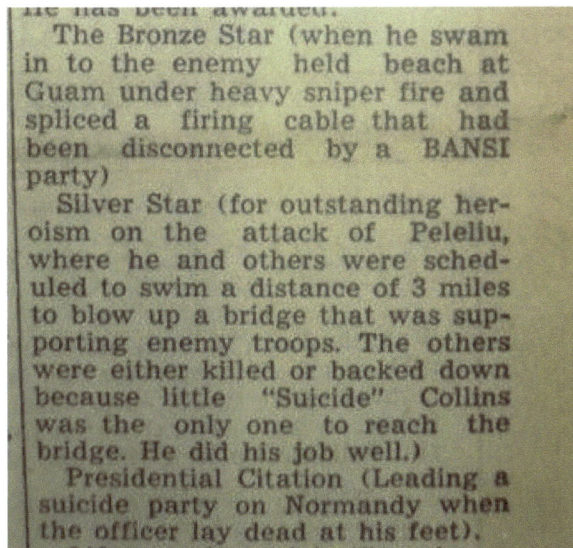

He has been awarded:
The Bronze Star (when he swam in to the enemy held beach at Guam under heavy sniper fire and spliced a firing cable that had been disconnected by a BANSI party)
Silver Star (for outstanding heroism on the attack of Peleliu, where he and others were scheduled to swim a distance of 3 miles to blow up a bridge that was supporting enemy troops. The others were either killed or backed down because little "Suicide" Collins was the only one to reach the bridge. He did his job well.)
Presidential Citation (Leading a suicide party on Normandy when the officer lay dead at his feet).

The Bronze Star (when he swam in to the enemy held beach at Guam under heavy sniper fire and spliced a firing cable that had been disconnected by a BANSI party)

Silver Star (for outstanding heroism on the attack of Pelellu, where he and others were scheduled to swim a distance of 3 miles to blow up a bridge that was supporting enemy troops. The others were either killed or backed down because little "Suicide" Collins was the only one to reach the bridge. He did his job well.")

Presidential Citation (Leading a suicide party on Normandy when the officer lay dead at his feet).

Life saver's medal, (Rescuing a drowning shipmate at Iwo Jima).

He has been recommended by Admiral William Halsey.

I recall a scene that took place on Tulagi (Solomans), a U.S.O. was entertaining the boys there and "Suicide's" face was plastered all over the front pages of all the West Coast papers, with stories of his ultra-impossible feats. The show consisted of Carole Landis, Jack Benny, Larry Adler and others. "suicide" was sitting down front and Miss Landis recognized him by his pictures. When the boys found that they had the "Lil" Poison" in their midst they went wild and nothing would do them but for Suicide to get up on the stage and play his Martin guitar and sing his famous "Tired."

He has been referred to by the leaders of our nation as "The Sergeant York" of World War II. His picture is now in the hall of fame along with Major Bong, Eddie Rickenbacker, Al Schmidt.

We all knew him as "Little Poison" and "Suicide" but after we got back to the States (what a reception turned out to see our boy" we had only been in dock about 15 minutes until he had his "little black book" full of blondes and red heads--and they bestowed upon him the name of "Octopus." No human could have so many hands. He is considered the catch of the year out in California and around. I could go on all day, gentlemen, but this bus gets to Blytheville soon and I wish to get this missive to you by all means. I believe he was known as "Blackie Collins" at Yorkville. He is Boatswains Mate First Class and he is now up for promotion. Thank you very much Gentlemen, Vice Admiral Brett Sheen.

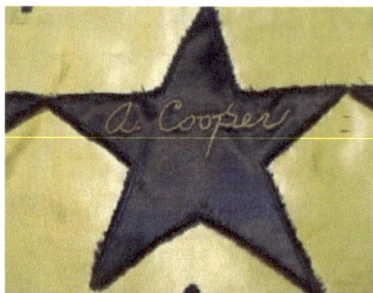

Cooper, A. [11]-Audrell Cooper; **CLASS OF 1934;** 9 February 1914-9 Sept 2006; buried in Yorkville [Find A Grave Memorial# 26579154]; son of John Thomas and Cora Gill

Cooper; 1930 District 8, Gibson County Census lists Audrell, age 16, with his parents and brothers: Waymon, age 21, Theo, age 12, and Robert, age 5. Husband of Ernestine Trout Cooper whom he married 24 December 1934 in Gibson County [His brother, Waymon Cooper served also.]

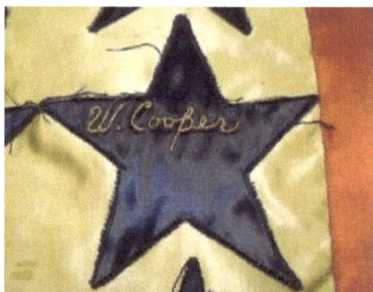

Cooper, W. [14]-Bernice Waymon Cooper; **CLASS OF 1929** 17 April 1909-20 June 1992; buried in Yorkville [Find A Grave Memorial# 26579239] : son of John Thomas and Cora Gill Cooper who married 7 Sept

1907 in Gibson County; 1910 District 8, Gibson County Census lists Bernis W., age 0, living with his parents; 1930 District 8, Gibson County Census lists Waymon, age 21, with his parents and brothers: Audrell, age 16; Theo, age 12, and Robert, age 5. Husband of Berenice Robinson Cooper whom he married 13 July 1939 in Dyer county; Enlisted 28 Jan 1943 in Army with 4 years High School; [brother, Audrell, also served] (note: the small picture is from the 1920-21 Yorkville School music class).

 *Listed on the Veteran's Memorial Listed as Bernice (1909) on http://www.fold3.com

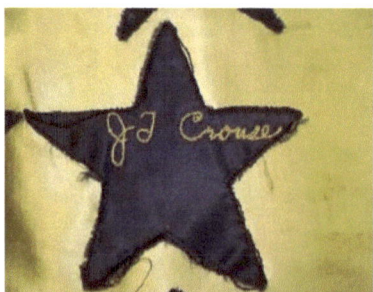

Crouse, J. T. [5]-James Tollie Crouse; 5 April 1927 to 15 September 2004; son of Russell E. and Liddie Fletcher Crouse who married 29 April 1926 in Gibson County ; 1940 Rural Gibson County Census lists Tollie, age 13, with his parents

Crowder, R. [1]-Ralph Crowder; son of Hammie Hubert and Grace Brown Crowder who married 7 October 1911 in Dyer County. 1930 District 8 Gibson county Census lists Ralph, age 10, living with his parents Hammie and Grace and brother, Lorence, age 14.

Culp, Ted [1]-Robert Alvin, Jr. "Ted" Culp; 12 Jan 1924 - 19 May 2011 Bremerton, Kitsap Co. Washington; buried in Arlington National Cemetery; [Find A Grave Memorial# 70364904]; son Robert Alvin and Florence Leggett Culp who married 21 Dec 1909 in Crockett County ; 1930 District 8 Gibson County Census lists Robert A, age 6, living with his parents.; 1940 Rural Gibson Co Census lists Ted Alvin, age 16, living with his parents.
His obituary states, "joined Navy at age 17 and his 20 year career took him around the world"

Davis, C. [9]-Chesley L. Davis; 1914; son of Drewery A. and Savana Neal Davis [Savana and Dewery A. are buried in the Yorkville Cemetery. Although no death date is inscribed for Dewery, his Gibson Death Certificate says 12 Jan 1953 and note: Dewery Tate, of Yorkville, age 62, married Lena Tate, age 34 in New Madrid, Missouri on 12 August 1941] 1920 Yorkville, Gibson County Census lists him as Chesley, age 5; 1940 Rural Gibson County Census lists C.L., age 26, 4th grade

OF THE FIVE YOUNG MEN IN THE CLASS OF 1938, FOUR SERVED IN THE MILITARY DURING WORLD WAR II.
VERLON BROWN, REUBEN LOGGINS
JAMES PARKER, JACK RAMSEY

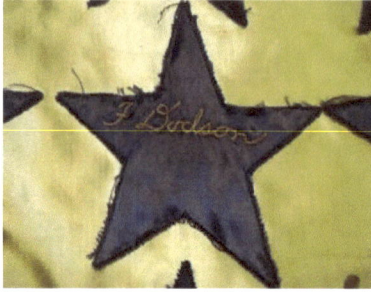

Dodson, F. [2] Freeman Richard Dodson; 24 April 1921-21 July 2001; buried in Yorkville [Find A Grave Memorial# 25346157]; son of Ezra James and Birtie May Fisher Dodson; 1940 Rural Gibson County Census lists Freeman, age 18, living with his parents.; Military Marker: M3 US Navy; served aboard the USS Chemung (AO 30)**); *Listed on the Veteran's Memorial** /Listed on fold3.com

Thanks to Karen Dodson Duncan for providing the military and family pictures of her father.

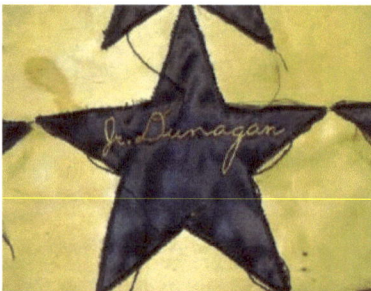

Dunagan, Jr. [7] Horace H. Dunagan, Jr. 20 Mar 1924-4 Feb 1987; buried in Caruthersville, Missouri [Find A Grave Memorial# 42150387] ; son of Horace Dunagan and Ruth Childress who married 22 Feb 1920 in Gibson County ; 1920 District 6 Gibson County Census lists Horace, age 6 with his parents; husband of Sara Zarecor, sister to Bob Zarecor, whom he married 10 Jan 1945 after his discharge 19 Oct 1944] Enlisted in the Navy 20 Mar 1941; **Listed on the Veterans' Memorial.**

*His baby sister, Kay, said that he served at Guadalcanal and in Australia. After serving in the Army in the Pacific Theatre, he returned to Yorkville High School and graduated with the **Class of 1947** were he served as Class President.*

[Jr. Dunagan continued] *In 1994, Marion Jetton wrote: "Do you remember Jr. Dunagan's return from the Navy and his adjustment and brave determination to get an education. How our giggles and restlessness must have annoyed him."*

[Interesting fact: Junior Dunagan's son, Dr. Nick Dunagan, would later serve as Chancellor of the University of Tennessee at Martin.]

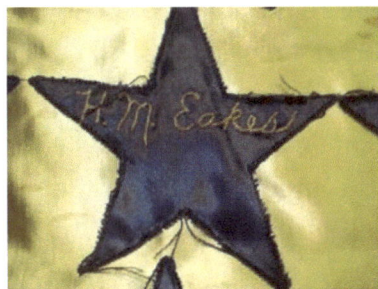

Eakes, H. M. [2]- born 14 August 1922 -19 July 1994 Riverdale, Clayton, Georgia; son of George Joseph "Joe" and Luda Fry Eakes who married 30 May 1909 Gibson county; 1930 District 8, Gibson County Census lists Wyatt, age 12, and H.M. ,age 7, is called Stan; 1940 Rural Gibson County census lists H. M. , age 17, living with his parents; enlisted in Army 24 December 1942 with 2 years High School; [Brothers H.M. and Wyatt both served]

Listed as H. M. Eakes on http://www.fold3.com

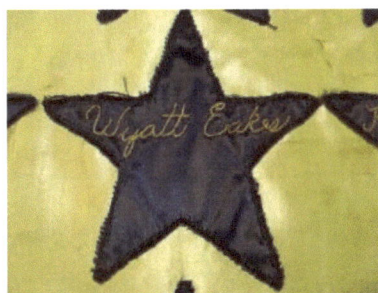

Eakes, Wyatt [11]-Class of 1936/Class President; 7 Dec 1917-21 Feb 1985 [Find A Grave Memorial# 7503844] son of George Joseph "Joe" and Luda Fry Eakes who married 30 May 1909 Gibson county; 1930 District 8, Gibson County Census lists Wyatt, age 12, and H.M. as Stan, age 7. [Brothers H.M. and Wyatt both served]

Wyatt Eakes
Vice Pres.

Edmiston, E.E. [5]-Edward Earl Edmiston; 19 May 1916-21 Aug 1965 [Find A Grave Memorial# 5355647] son of Michael David and Effie Lula Boyett Edmiston who married 22 Feb 1903 in Gibson County; husband of Eva Letha Wilson Edmiston ; 1930 Rutherford Gibson county census lists Edward E, age 13 and Roy F, age 11, living with their parents.; Enlisted Army 16 Oct 1940 with 1 year high school from Dyer County; [Brothers: Roy Fay served in WWII also]

Listed as Edward E Edmiston with his birth as 1917on http://www.fold3.com

Edmiston, R. F. (Gold Star) [4] Roy Fay Edmiston; 8 November 1919-28 Dec 1943 Trinidad and Tobago (death was from an infection while on board the ship, not battle) ; son of Michael David and Effie Lula Boyett Edmiston who married 22 Feb 1903 in Gibson County; 1930 Rutherford Gibson county census lists Edward E, age 13 and Roy F, age 11, living with their parents.; [Brother, Edward Earl, served in WWII also]; husband of Martha Ann Hall Edmiston whom he married 28 March 1941 in Dyer County; Enlisted US Navy 17 Feb 1940; served aboard U.S.S. St. Louis. His last muster roll for 31 Dec 1943 listed him aboard USS SC 1298 with his destination as Nashville, Tennessee. ***Listed on the Special section of the Veteran's Memorial for those who made the supreme sacrifice.**

"Dies Overseas-Roy Fay Edmiston, gunners mate first class of the Navy, died Dec. 29 of a heart ailment overseas while in the service of his country, his wife Mrs. Martha Ann Edmiston, of Newbern, Tenn., was informed Monday. He also leaves and infant daughter, his father, Ike Edmiston of near Newbern, a sister, Mrs. J. D. Cook of Dyersburg, and three brothers, Merritt of Dyer, Hickman of near Newbern and Edward Earl Edmiston of the Army in England."

Thanks to Sue Edmiston Lynn, Roy's brother Hickman's daughter, for providing pictures. Roy Fay stands with his wife, Martha Ann Hall Edmiston. Note: The daughter, Sherry, was born about 1943.

Roy Fay Edmiston, gunners mate first class of the Navy, died Dec. 29 of a heart ailment overseas while in the service of his country, his wife, Mrs. Martha Ann Edmiston, of Newbern, Tenn., was informed Monday. He also leaves an infant daughter, his father, Ike Edmiston of near Newbern, a sister, Mrs. J. D. Cook of Dyersburg, and three brothers, Merritt of Dyer, Hickman of near Newbern and Edward Earl Edmiston of the Army in England.

A TRIBUTE TO ROY FAY EDMISTON AND HARRY WILSON JONES

After the War, the Yorkville Cumberland Presbyterian Church dedicated a Hammond

IN MEMORY OF:

Lt. Harry Wilson Jones, who was born to the union of Mr. W.F. Jones and Mrs. Hortens Jones near Yorkville November 9, 1916. He attended the local schools until his graduation from the High School in 1935. He attended the University of Tennessee and graduated there in 1940. When a child of 10 he united with the Cumberland Presbyterian Church.

Lt. Jones served with the Marines and was noted for his bravery and pride in his unit. He was mortally wounded and died on February 25, 1945.

AND

Roy Fay Edmiston, Gunner's Mate 1st. Class, who was born to the union of Mr. Michael Edmiston and Mrs. Effie Edmiston November 8, 1918. He attended the local grade and high schools faithfully. Early in life he united with the Cumberland Presbyterian Church. On march 28, 1941 he was united in marriage to Martha Ann Hall and to this union Sherria Fay was born.

Roy Fay Edmiston gave his life for his country and those who loved him are justly proud that he served his God and Country with commendable devotion and loyalty.

****

It is fitting that we honor their memory with the celestial music produced on the instrument given in their honor.

IN MEMORY OF
HARRY WILSON JONES — ROY FAY EDMISTON

Organ in Memory of Gunner's Mate 1st Class Roy Fay Edmiston and Lt. Harry Wilson Jones who had attended the church. Both boys had united with the church at an early age.

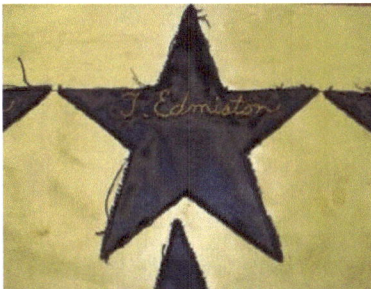

Edmiston, Theron[6] Theron Hal Edmiston **CLASS OF 1932**; 25 August 1913- 20 July 1993 in Martin; buried Cool Springs Cumberland Presbyterian Cemetery [Find A Grave Memorial# 51759689] son of Edd Smith and Lessie Johnson Edmiston who married 23 Nov 1912 Gibson County; 1920 Yorkville, Gibson County Census lists Theron, age 6, living with his parents. Enlisted in the US Navy 20 Nov 1940 in Nashville; Served aboard the USS Bosditch (AG30). [See YHS Basketball picture on p. 37.]

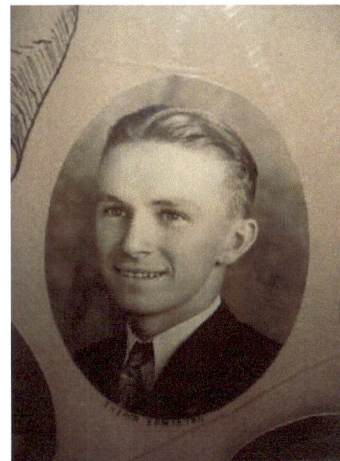

Listed as Theron H Edmiston on www.fold3.com [note: only man by that name!]

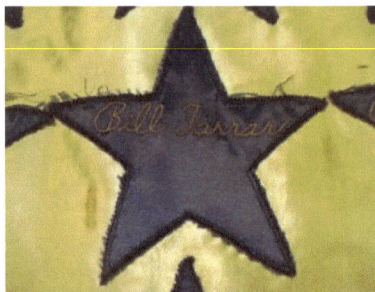

Farrar, Bill [12]-William Lee Farrar; **CLASS OF 1927 (composite picture unavailable);** 18 March 1909-5 Jan 1972 Silver Springs, Maryland; son of Luther and Sammie Loggins Farrar who married 30 Nov 1906 in Gibson County; brother to H.L. Farrar who also served; husband to Opal Crabtree Farrar whom he married on 7 December 1941 in Washington, D.C.; Enlisted 29 September 1943 at Ft. Myers, Virginia with 4 years High School, married and a salesman

*Listed on the Veteran's Memorial

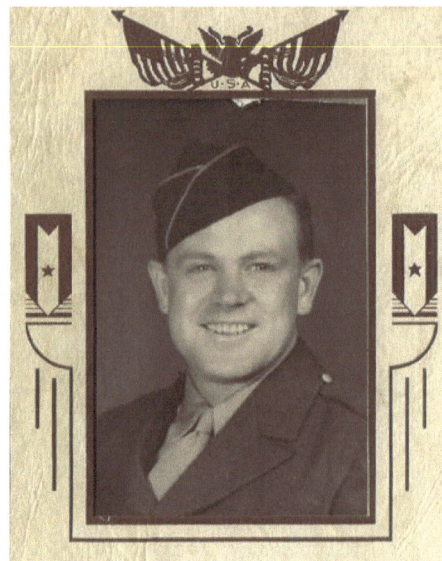

His daughter, Sharon Farrar Krieger, related that her parents told her of the Bombing of Pearl Harbor on their wedding day. Sharon provided the Class of 1927 information. This picture, in its original military frame, belonged to his mother, Sammie Loggins Farrar and his sister, Addie Eola "Adiola" Farrar Cowan. H.L. "Sonny" Farrar, Jr. provided me with the picture.

THE YORKVILLE HIGH SCHOOL CLASS OF 1927 GRADUATION PROGRAM LISTING BILL FARRAR AND ALLINE HARRIS

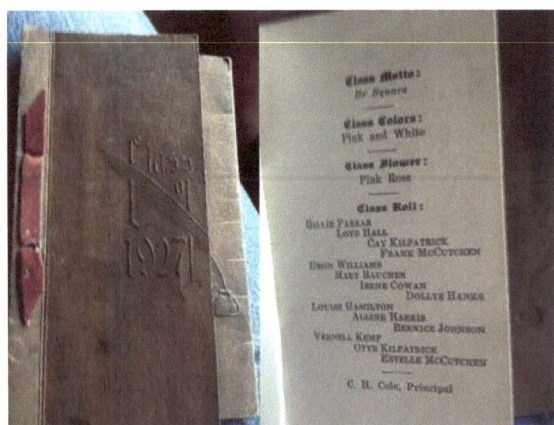

Class Members: **Billie Farrar**, Loyd Hall, Cay Kilpratick, Frank McCutchen, Eron Williams, Mary Baucher, Irene Cowen, Dollye Hanks, Louise Hamilton, **Alline Harris,** Bernice Johnson, Vernell Kemp, Otye Kilpatrick, Estelle McCutchen   Principal: C.H. Cole

Farrar, H. L. [12]- Henry Lafayette Farrar **CLASS OF 1925 [composite picture not available];** 20 Sept 1907-24 August 1970 Silver Springs, Maryland [Findagrave #44383281]; son of Luther and Sammie Loggins Farrar who married 30 Nov 1906 in Gibson county; enlisted 28 Sept 1943 in the Army with 4 years High School in Washington, D.C. ***Listed on the Veteran's Memorial.** (note: He is the father of Henry Lafayette "Sonny" Farrar, Jr.); brothers H.L. and Bill Farrar both served in the Army during World War II.   Listed as Henry L Farrar on www. fold3.com

Picture from the photograph collection of Henry's Uncle Reuben Wilson Loggins, Sr.

The following is Stamped on the back: **MEDICAL PHOTOGRAPHY DEPARTMENT** U.S.Naval Medical School National Naval Medical Center Bethesda 14, Maryland

H.L. "Henry" Farrar, Sr. continued to serve the Military and their families after the war. He wore a "slightly" different uniform. The "baby boomers" of the Yorkville Community benefited from his "service," too.

Karen (Dodson) Duncan and John Robert McCaffrey pose with Santa at the Yorkville Cumberland Presbyterian Church.

Flatt, Charles [13] Charles Edward Flatt; 25 July 1923-17 Jan 2012; buried in the Chattanooga National Cemetery [Find A Grave Memorial# 95856371] son of William Thomas and Cattie Morrow Flatt, Jr. who married 8 October in Dyer County ; 1930 District 9, Dyer County census lists Verne Flatt, age 8, and Charles Flatt, age 6, living with their parents; Military inscription on marker: CPL US Army World War II; Brothers Charles and Vern both served.

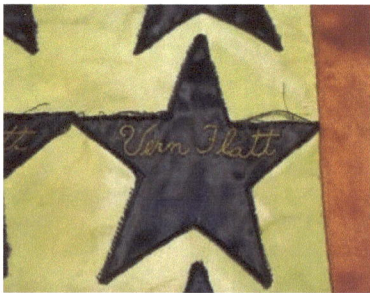

Flatt, Vern [14] James Vern Flatt; **CLASS OF 1940;** son of William Thomas and Virginia Catherine "Cattie "Morrow Flatt, Jr. who married 8 October in Dyer County; 1930 District 9, Dyer County census lists Verne Flatt, age 8, and Charles Flatt, age 6, living with their parents; 1941 University of Tennessee at Knoxville Year book lists him as James Vern Flatt, Class of 1944.

Bettye Loggins says that Vern was tall, about 6'5", and a great basketball player on the Yorkville High School Team.

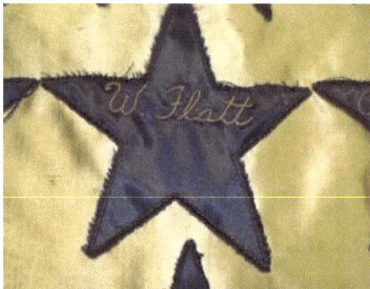

Flatt, W. [3]-Wilburn D. Flatt; 16 March 1925- 15 Apr 1997 Chicago, Illinois; son of James Madison and Clara Gibbon Flatt; 1930 District 8 Census lists Wilburn, age 5, living with his parents.; 1940 Rural Gibson County Census, (Bells Chapel Community) lists Wilbur, age 14, living with his parents.; enlisted Army 25 June 1943 with 2 years High School

Listed as Wilburn D. Flatt on http://www.fold3.com

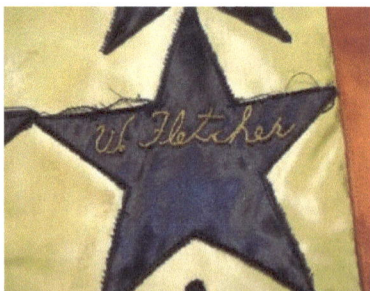

Fletcher, W. [14]- William Fletcher; born about 1923; son of Tollie and Ada Litton Fletcher who married 1 Sept 1907 in Gibson County; 1930 District 8 Gibson County census lists William, age 8, living with his parents.; 1940 Rural Gibson County census lists William, age 17, living with his parents.

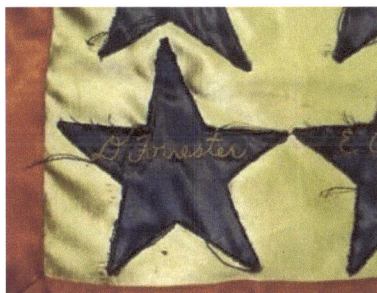

Forrester, D. [1] Thomas Derwood Forrester; **Class of 1937;** 4 August 1918-30 April 1970; buried in Fairview Cemetery in Newbern [Find A Grave Memorial# 63711538], (little fact: He had a twin brother, Sherwood, who graduated in the same class); son of John M. and Edna Moore Forrester who married 28 Feb 1901 in Dyer County; 1920 Civil District 8 lists Thomas D Forrester, age 1, living with his parents. [note: twin brother is listed as Hugh S.]; 1930 District 8, Dyer County Census lists Derwood and Sherwood, age 11, living with their brother James and his wife because both parents are deceased.; enlisted 10 Feb 1942 in Georgia with 4 years High School as a private. He listed his occupation as salesman.

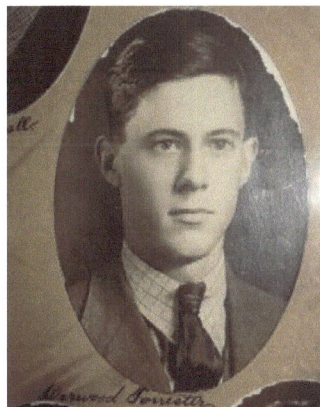

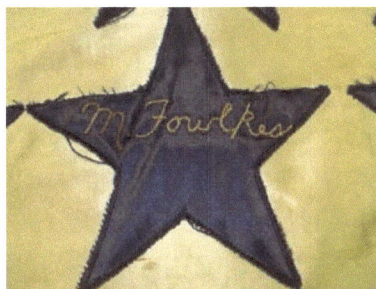

Fowlkes, M. [9]-Marshall C. Fowlkes; 6 July 1920-10 April 2005; buried in the Cool Springs Cumberland Presbyterian Cemetery [Find A Grave Memorial# 96398112 and Find A Grave Memorial# 98412368] son of Aubrey M. and Virginia Carroll Fowlkes who married 15 Jan 1915 in Dyer county; 1930 District 9 Gibson County Census lists Marshall, age 10, with his parents.; Military inscription: F 1, U.S. Navy, WW II. from the U.S. Dept of Veteran's Affairs (note: F1 means Commander-in-Chief, Plans Division (USN)

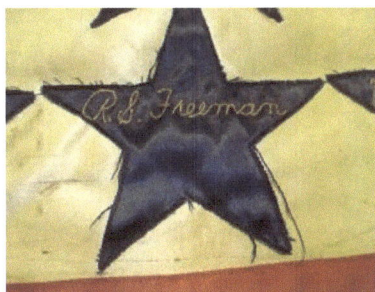

Freeman, R. S. [11]- Robert Shanon Freeman, Jr. 13 December 1922-4 November 1973, buried in Oakwood in Dyer [Find A Grave Memorial# 15632487]; son of Robert Shanon and Ima Wallace who married 13 August 1917 in Gibson County; 1930 District 6 Gibson county census lists Robert S. with his parents.; 1940 Rural Gibson County Census lists R.S., age 17, living with his parents. ***Listed on the Veteran's Memorial.** According to his daughter, Denise, he served in the Navy.

[Little Fact: R.S. Freeman served as the Field Representative for United States Congressman Ed Jones]

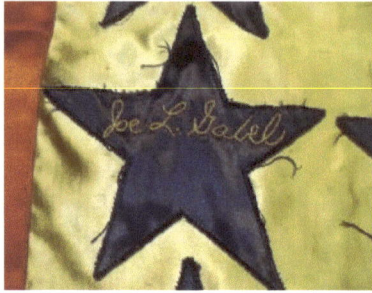

Gabel, Joe L. [1] Joel Aaron Gabel; 7 September 1919-11 November 2006; buried North Union Cumberland Presbyterian Church Cemetery [Find A Grave Memorial# 100198696] son of Frank B. and Ellie Hanks Gabel who married 13 March 1926 in Gibson County; husband of Martha Elouise Page of Trimble whom he married 14 Dec. 1942 in Caruthersville, Pemiscot, Missouri; Information from Navy Muster Rolls: Enlisted Nashville 6 Dec 1939 in the Navy, Served aboard the USS Saratoga beginning 8 March 1940, Transferred from the USS Saratoga (CV-3) to Fighting Squadron 2 on 6 May 1940,   Received US Naval Hospital Pearl Harbor on 28 Feb 1942, Received 22 Feb 1942 from Fighting Squadron 2, rank AMM2c (#295 53 82 He was then transferred back to Fighting Squadron 2 on 25 May 1942, Received on board the USS Solomons (CVE67) 21 Nov 1943 with rank AMM1c , Promoted aboard 16 Feb 1945 the USS Solomons to [Aviation Chief Machinist's Mate, Gas Turbine Mechanic] Listed as Joe E. Galloway on http://www.fold3.com

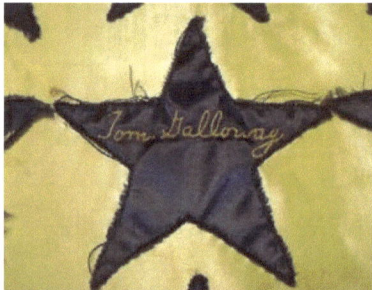

Galloway, Tom [11]-Thomas J. Galloway; 25 November 1924-21 August 2001 in Montana; buried in Yorkville [Find A Grave Memorial# 25348583]; S1 US NAVY; son of Thomas Wesley and Mary Rowdon Galloway who married 12 November 1907 in Lewis County, TN; 1930 District 8 Gibson County Census lists Thomas J., age 9, and Joe, age 5, with their parents.; [brother Joe E. in WWII also] Military marker: S1 US NAVY; ***Listed on the Veteran's Memorial**

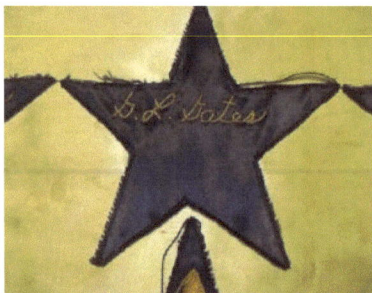

Gates, G.L. [7]-Glynn Latimer "Shorty" Gates; **CLASS OF 1936;** 30 Jan 1918-28 Jan 1990; buried in Yorkville [Find A Grave Memorial# 18995904] son of Robert W. and Lelia Florence Ramsey Gates; S Sgt US Army; 1940 France Field, Cristobal, Panama Canal Census lists him as in US Army; (US WWII Enlistment records had incorrect birth date of 1862 when searched 8 April 2014. It was corrected.) enlisted 8 Jan 1940 from Gibson Co. with post graduate education; Listed as Glynn L Gates on http://www.fold3.com ***Listed on the Veteran's Memorial as Glenn L. Gates**

Glvn L. Gates

Grantham R. A. [5]-Robert Allen Grantham; 28 Nov 1921-22 Jan 2007 Yukon, Oklahoma; [Find A Grave Memorial# 43800428]; son of Allen and Pearlie Leigh Luckett Grantham who married 22 February 1920 in Obion County;1940 Memphis, Shelby County Census lists Robert A Grantham, age 18, with an inferred Rural Dyer County residence in 1935. He is living with his grandmother, Louise Grantham. 1930 District 9 Obion County Census lists Robert A , age 8, living with his mother and father. (The obituary Daily Times had this entry: GRANTHAM, Robert Allen; 85; Obion Co TN>Yukon OK; Daily Oklahoman; 2007-2-2; ccc);

According Wenzel Family Tree on Ancestry.com, he married Marian Hazel Dennis on 19 August 1944 in Oklahoma City, Oklahoma. The military picture with his wife was originally posted to his page in this tree by Jane Wenzel.

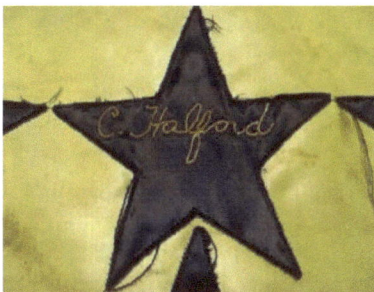

Halford, C. [10]- Marion Carlton Harford; **Class of 1934** 10 March 1914-24 October 1998; buried Sunnyside in Kenton [Find A Grave Memorial# 107791353]; son of Ira E and Nettie E. Whitley Halford who were married in 1913 in Gibson county; Military Marker: S SGT US ARMY WORLD WAR II; enlisted 25 June 1941 from Gibson County in Army as a private with 4 yrs high school; ***M.C. Halford is listed on Veteran's Memorial**;

His son Curtis says that his dad served in the Pacific Theater in the Philippines and New Guinea.

Who was responsible for the mail in and out of Yorkville during WWII? According to <u>Gibson County Past and Present</u>, Mr. Cleo Pipkin began serving as Postmaster of Yorkville in 1918. He served until his death on December 31, 1945.

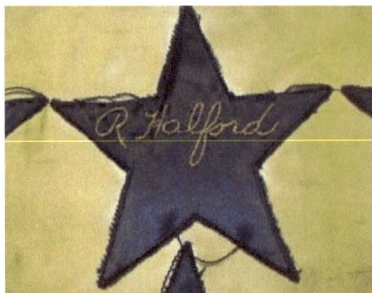

Halford, R. [8]-Raymond Halford; 3 July 1922- 25 September 1998 Union City; son of John Harrison and Quincy Smithwick Halford who married 19 Dec 1919 in Gibson County; 1930 District 8, Gibson County Census, Raymond, age 7, is living with his parents and older brother, Malcolm, age 13; 1940 Rural Gibson County Census lists Raymond, age 17, living with parents. [Brother Malcolm T. Halford serves in the Navy during WWII and then makes the Navy his career.] *10 January 1956 TRI-CITY REPORTER: "Raymond Halford reenlisted in the Navy and left for Nashville this week."*

Hall, Guy [13] CLASS OF 1937; Guy H. Hall; 20 January 1919-9 August 1993 in St. Louis, Missouri; son of Marvin and Winnie Parnell Hall who married 12 Dec 1917 in Dyer County;1920 District 9 Dyer County Census lists James and Guy Hall, age 11/12 months, living with their parents; 1930 District 9 Dyer County Census lists James and Guy Hall, age 11, living with their parents; 1940 St. Louis, St. Louis City, Missouri Census has Guy H. and James P. Hall living with their uncle, James M. Hall, with an inferred residence for 1935 in Rural Gibson County, Tennessee**.; *Listed on the Veteran's Memorial;**[Twin brother to James Hall]

Hall, James [14]-James Wilson Hall; **CLASS OF 1937;** 20 Jan 1919-16 May 1967; buried in Yorkville [Find A Grave Memorial# 25385239]; son of Marvin and Winnie Parnell Hall who marred 12 Dec 1917 in Dyer County;1920 District 9 Dyer County Census lists James and Guy Hall, age 11/12 months, living with their parents; 1930 District 9 Dyer County Census lists James and Guy Hall, age 11, living with their parents; 1940 St. Louis, St. Louis City, Missouri Census has

Guy H. and James P. Hall living with their uncle, James M. Hall, with an inferred residence for 1935 in Rural Gibson County, Tennessee.; military marker: T Sgt 373 General Hosp; ***Listed on the Veteran's Memorial** [Twin brother to Guy Hall]

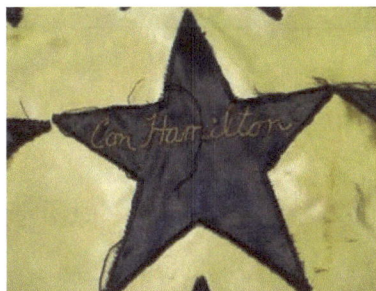

Hamilton, Con[13]-Con Dudley Hamilton, Jr.; **CLASS OF 1934; 14** Feb. 1917-2 Nov 1990 Cleburne, Texas ; son of Con Dudley and Vonnie Vera King Hamilton, Sr. who married 30 April 1914 in Gibson County; 1920 District 8 Gibson county census lists Con Dudley, age 2 11/12, living with his parents. 1930 District 8, Gibson County Census lists Con, age 13, and Harold, age 7, living with their parents; Husband of Vivian May Basinger [Information from Vivian's Find A Grave Memorial# 14267626; whom he met while in medical school. They married 7 November 1940 in Bolivar. She is from Indiana.; brother Harold is also serving in WWII.; ***Listed on the Veteran's Memorial**

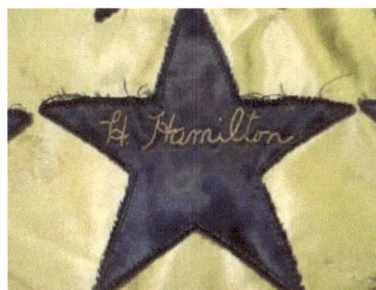

Hamilton, H. [12]-Harold Hamilton; **Class of 1939**; born 27 October 1921-13 May 1998 Tuscumbia, Alabama; son of Con Dudley and Vonnie Vera King Hamilton who married 30 April 1913 in Gibson County; 1930 District 8, Gibson County Census lists Con, age 13, and Harold, age 7, living with their parents; 1940 Rural Gibson County Census lists Harold, age 18, with his parents. Brother to Con Hamilton who also served. Attended the University of Tennessee at Knoxville and was listed in the 1940 yearbook as Class of 1943. ***Listed on the Veteran's Memorial**

One of the courses that the young men of YHS took was Agriculture. During the formative years of many of these young men, Melvin Isaac Revelle was the teacher. Even though he was known for his "coal shovel" of discipline, he was well loved and respected. In addition to teaching, Mr. Revelle was very active in the Yorkville Cattle Show and as an Elder in the Yorkville Cumberland Presbyterian Church.

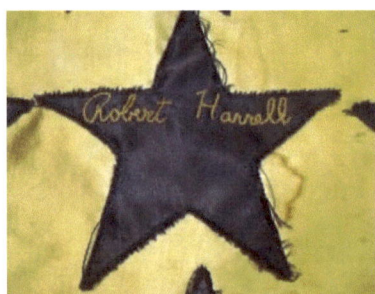

M.I. Revelle
Agriculture

Harrell, Robert [5]-Robert Couch Harrell; **CLASS OF 1937;** 23 July 1918-28 Oct 1999; Buried in Yorkville [Find A Grave Memorial# 18630922]; son of Robert Lee and Myrtie Ann Couch Harrell who married 13 November 1913 in Gibson County; 1920 District 8 Census lists Robert Couch, age 1 6/12, living with his parents; husband of Inez Ladd Harrell whom he married 9 Feb 1941 in Dyer County; enlisted 9 June 1944 in Army with 4 years high school; *Listed on the Veteran's Memorial

Listed as Robert C Harrell on http://www.fold3.com

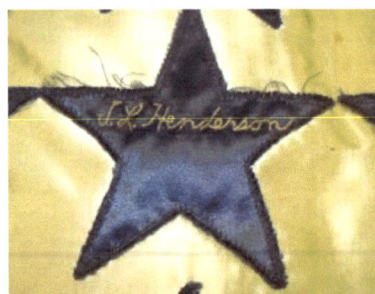

Robert Harrell

Henderson, J.L. [11]-John L. Henderson; **Class of 1932** birth 1914; James L. "Jim" and Effie Wambley Henderson (1920 Rutherford Gibson Co Census has James L as father, Effie as mother, and sister, Louise; 1930 District 8 Gibson Co Census listed as John L. age 15, with Jim Henderson, born 1864, and Effie Henderson, age 56; 1940 Memphis, Shelby County Census lists John, age 25, with Effie as mother, age 67, and Louise as sister, age 31); enlisted 4 March 1943 in Shelby Co. in the army with 2 years of college

Listed as John L Henderson, born 1914 on www.fold3.com

During World War II, the practice of displaying a service flag became widespread and it is reported that virtually every home or organization displayed banners with a star for each person serving in the military. The Blue Star represented hope and pride. When the family lost the family member to the war effort, they covered the blue star with a gold one that represented sacrifice to the cause of liberty and freedom. [The picture is a section of a WWII poster that was labeled "because someone talked."]

Jackson, J. [13] Jamie E. Jackson; CLASS OF 1942; son of Horace Armon and Laura Fay McKnight Jackson who married 6 May 1922 in Gibson County; Jamie, age 7, is listed in 1930 District 15 Dyer County Census listed with parents, Horace A. and Laura Fay Jackson with sisters,

Rebecca and Jocelyn; 1940 Rural Gibson County Census list Jamie with parents and sisters.; Enlisted in the Army 25 January 1943

His son, Danny who is a Viet Nam (1967-1968) veteran, said that his father was in the Army in the Americal Division [note: 23rd Infantry Division] in the Pacific Theatre. He fought in the Philippines and was staged to go to Japan when the war ended. He served with the Occupational Forces in Japan. ***Listed on the Veteran's Memorial**

Listed as Jamie E Jackson on www.fold3.com

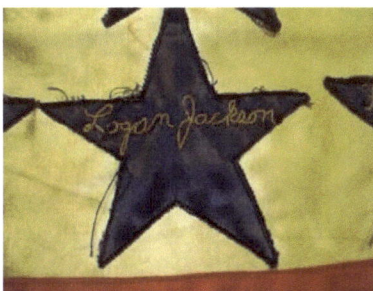

Jackson, Logan [3]- Logan C. A. Jackson; 1921-1976; buried at Cool Springs Cumberland Presbyterian Church [Find A Grave Memorial# 98412520]; son of Charles A and Lettie Minton Jackson who married in 1919 in

Gibson County; 1930 District 24 Gibson co. census lists Logan, age 9, living with his parents; 1940 Gibson county Census lists Logan C A, age 19, living with his parents. enlisted in Army 24 Dec 1942 in Shelby County with 3 years High School

Listed as Logan C A Jackson on www.fold3.com

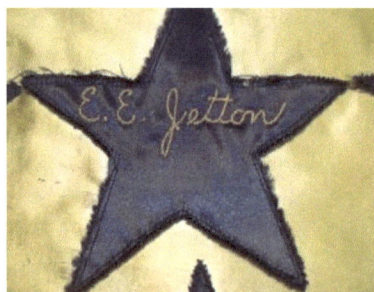

Jetton, E.E. [4]-Emerson Ethridge "Tony" Jetton; **CLASS OF 1936**: 17 Dec 1917-Sept 2010 New Mexico; buried in Union City [Find A Grave Memorial# 59474529]; son of John Louis and Harlan Couch Jetton who were married 22 Dec 1916 in

Emerson E. Jetton

Gibson County; 1920 Civil District 8 Gibson County Census lists Emerson Ethridge, age 2, living with his parents. 1930 District 8 Gibson County census lists Emerson, age 12, and J.L., age 6, living with their parents; Enlisted in the Navy 4 Oct 1943 in New Mexico; served aboard the USS Cachalot (SS 170); rank: McMM2c (T) [Brother John Louis, Jr. also served]

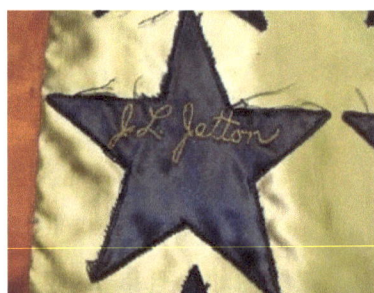

Jetton, J.L. [1]- John Louis Jetton, Jr.; born 7 Feb 1922-March 1979 Shelby County; son of John Louis and Harlan Couch Jetton who were married 22 Dec 1916 in Gibson County; 1930 District 8 Gibson County census lists Emerson, age 12, and J.L., age 6, living with their parents.[brother Emerson Ethridge Jetton also served]

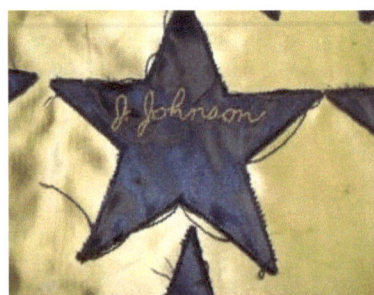

Johnson, J. [2]-Jesse L. Johnson, Jr. ; May 1927-5 November 1995; buried in Yorkville [Find A Grave Memorial# 111468452]; ; son of Jesse Lamb and Georgia Vestal Gray Johnson, Sr who married 1 Dec 1916 in Dyer County; 1930 District 8 Gibson co census lists Jesse, age 3 1/12, living with his parents; enlisted 14 September 1945 in Army with a grammar school education: ***Listed on the Veteran's Memorial**

Listed as Jesse L. Johnson, Jr . on http://www.fold3.com

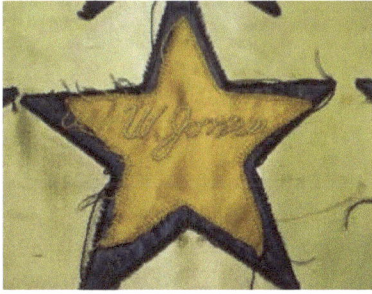

Jones, W. (gold star) [7]-Harry Wilson Jones; **Class of 1936** 9 November 1916-25 Feb 1945 Motoyma Airfield Number Two, Iwo Jima; KIA; buried in Yorkville [Find A Grave Memorial# 111295325] Lieutenant in U.S. Marine Corps; son of Will F. "Gabe" and Hortense Pipkin Jones who married 14 June 1910 in Gibson County; ***Listed on the Special section of the Veteran's Memorial for those who made the supreme sacrifice.**

Wilson Jones—President

> *Paper dated 7 June 1945: "Memorial Service for Wilson Jones to be held Sunday--Sunday afternoon, June 10, at 3 o'clock, friends of Lieut. Wilson Jones, who was killed in action on Iwo Jima, Feb. 25, will gather at the Yorkville Cumberland Presbyterian Church for a Memorial Service in his honor. Rev. Lon Brewer, pastor of the church will conduct the service.*
>
> *Lieut. Jones, youngest son of Mr. and Mrs. W. F. Jones of Yorkville, was born Nov. 9, 1916. From his early boyhood, he had an intense interest in Jersey cattle and was regarded as one of the outstanding young dairymen of the South. He was manager of the Ridgeway Jersey Farms at Athens, Tenn., when he went into service.*
>
> *'He had certainly accomplished a lot for a person of his age.' I. O. Colebank, of the State Extension Service, said upon learning of his death."*

Listed as Harry Wilson Jones and Lt. Harry Wilson Jones on http://www.fold3.com

---

Somewhere in the South Pacific, July 22--A main road in the Ninth Regiment of the Third Marine Division has been named "Jones Street" in honor of Marine Lieut. Harry Wilson Jones, who was killed on Iwo Jima. Lieutenant Jones was the son of W. F. Jones, Yorkville, Tenn and had been overseas for 18 months when he was fatally wounded Feb. 25, 1945. A veteran of Bougainville and Guam campaigns, Lieutenant Jones won the Bronze Star Medal for valor in the latter operation. He had led a rifle outfit in a successful attack on a Jap stronghold which was impending an advance of a vital Guam airfield. Lieutenant Jones underwent an operation at Pearl Harbor last December but recovered in time to rejoin his outfit as it embarked for Iwo Jima. While leading a platoon against the enemy, near Motoyma Airfield Number Two, Lieutenant Jones was hit by artillery fire and died shortly thereafter. In dedicating the Street, Ninth Regiment Commanding Officer, Col. Howard N. Kenyon, said in part: "Lieutenant Jones was an intrepid Marine and a skillful leader. He fought valiantly at Bougainville, Guam, and Iwo Jima. He is gone but the memory of his brave deeds and devotion to duty will live with his men who remain to continue the fight against the Japanese forces."

26 July 1945 TRI-CITY REPORTER

Harry Wilson Jones Articles

Expressions of Eulogy

"He had certainly accomplished a lot for a person of his age, and I don't believe that there is a young man in the State with more friends."

..... Mr. L. O. Colebank, Agricultural
Extension Service.

———o———

"The Jersey Fraternity has lost a real man, yet, we all will be strengthened by the fact that Wilson Jones was among us, though but for an all too brief span of time."

... Mr. W. R. Cooke,
Ridgeway Farms.

———o———

"I shall never forget Wilson. He was magnificent in every respect; the sort of person I'd like to be if I could become young again."

.... Dr. J. B. Naive, Supt.
Beverly Hills Sanatorium

———o———

"Many of us can live twice or three times as long and not leave as much."

.... Mr. Harry Marsh

———o———

"I was Wilson's battalion commander during the hellish Iwo Jima campaign and can only say that in him the Marine Corps has lost an outstanding officer and an all-round, grand young man."

.... Lieutenant Colonial Harold C. Boehm.

———o———

"We will miss him as one of our outstanding alumni in the College of Agriculture of the University of Tennessee."

.... Mr. C. E. Wylie,
Department of Dairying

The Rev. Lon Brewer, his pastor, used for the subject of his sermon, "Going Home to God." Miss Peggy Jean Dozier sang "Going Home." M. L. Reville, vocational agricultural teacher and secretary of the Yorkville Jersey Cattle Club, said Wilson Jones showed ability to judging and raising Jerseys even as a boy and was a good showman in high school days. He recalled that Wilson Jones was a member of the Scarabbean Society while a senior in the University of Tennessee and also a member of the Alpha Zeta fraternity, a national honorary agriculture fraternity.

Mr. Reville said Mr. Jones worked on the Ridgeway Farms at Athens during college days, and made the dairy herds of that farm famous after he graduated from the university. Because of this important work he need not have gone to war, but felt it his duty and volunteered, fighting with the Third Marine Corps. His parents are Mr. and Mrs. W. F. Jones of Yorkville.

21 June 1945
COURIER
CHRONICLE

1935 Yorkville Boys Basket Ball Team.
Wilson Jones is the first boy on the left.

Lieut. Owen of the Marines, of the Millington Air Base, spent a few days in Yorkville recently, and presented Mr. and Mrs. W. F. Jones with a Citation and Bronze Star in memory of the heroic work of their son, the late Wilson Jones.

30 May 1946 TRI-CITY REPORTER

The Charter for Thompson-Jones, Post 3765 of the Veterans of Foreign Wars is flanked by the pictures of the young men for whom it was named. The Post was located in Dyer, Tennessee. Post 3765 is no longer active but the building is now owned and maintained by the city of Dyer, Tennessee.

The Yorkville Jersey Cattle Show

Starting with the first show in 1929, the Yorkville Jersey Cattle Show, held in August, began bringing large numbers of people to the community of Yorkville. Mr. Will "Gabe" Jones, who was the father of *Harry Wilson Jones [WWII Gold Star Veteran]*; Mr. Frank Vaughn, who was the father of *Wilber Vaughn [WWII Veteran]*; and Mr. Opie Pope were the primary directors for years.

According to the 26 August 1943 HERALD RESGISTER article, the grandfather of *Ewing Wyatt [World War II Veteran]*, Dr. A. E. Turner, was the first person to introduce the Jersey cow to Gibson County. The author of the article reported this about Ewing's uncle, Banks Turner: "He remembers this cow very well. Her name was Millie, and when people came to look at the rich yellow butter produced from Millie's milk, most of them insisted that the butter had been artificially colored."

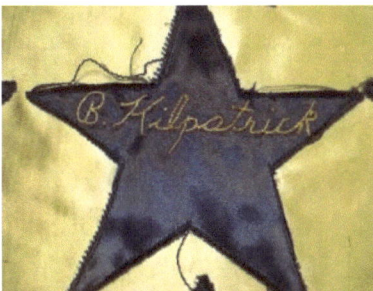

Kilpatrick, B. [3]-Brodie H. Kilpatrick ; **Class of 1937** 15 Jan 1917-26 Oct 2009; buried in Memphis Memorial Park [Find A Grave Memorial# 105707414]; son of Cleveland Needham and Jennie May (maiden name) Kilpatrick who married 12 March 1905 in Gibson County ; 1920 District 24 Gibson Co: Brodie Kilpatrick, age 3 with widowed mother, Jennie Kilpatrick; enlisted 23 January 1941 with 4 yrs HS and released 29 Sep 1945; From his obituary " proudly served in WW II in 117th Army Infantry, known as the Break Through Regiment." Listed as Brodie Kilpatrick (1917) and as Brodie H. Kilpatrick on http://www.fold3.com

YORKVILLE CLASS HOLDS REUNION AT REELFOOT

The Senior Class of 1937, alumni of Yorkville High School, held its first annual meeting and reunion at Reelfoot Lake Wednesday, June 1. The day was spent in conversing and recalling school days together. A bountiful lunch was spread at the noon hour, after which several enjoyed a swim in the lake. Miss Wylodean King was elected secretary and treasurer for the coming year, succeeding Miss Geneva Crawford. A poem, composed by Geneva Crawford, in memory of a deceased classmate, Miss Willie Maude Ladd, was read to the class.

Fourteen of the nineteen members of the class attended. Those present were: Misses Katherine Flatt, Opal Hanks, Wylodean King, Laura Mae Crawford, Geneva Crawford, Claudine Childress, Mrs. Georgia Lee Trice McKeel, and Messrs Robert Harrell, Ralph Crowder, James Hall, Derwood Forrester, Sherwood Forrester, Farris Austin, and Herbert Kuykendall. Mrs. Jewel P. Smith, sponsor of the class, also attended. Guests were Miss Sena Trumbell, of Blytheville, Ark., and Robert Hulme, of Newbern.

This Reunion was held before the War.

THE CLASS OF 1937 HAD THE HIGHEST NUMBER OF YOUNG MEN TO SERVE IN WORLD WAR II.

FARRIS AUSTIN, SHERWOOD FORRESTER, GUY HALL, JAMES HALL, ROBERT HARRELL, BRODIE KILPATRICK, HERBERT KUYKENDALL, HARRY PARKS WILSON

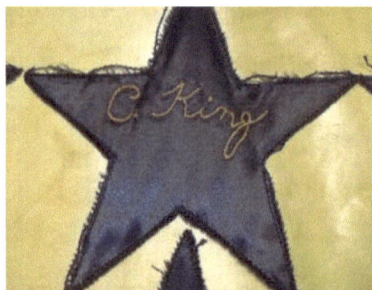

King, C. [11] James Cecil King; 9 July 1921-25 June 2006; Buried in Oakwood in Dyer [Find A Grave Memorial# 15784159] son of David B. and Ozella Garner King who married 22 Dec 1918 in Gibson County; enlisted in the Navy 30 August 1940 (service #295 73 29) and came aboard the USS Pennsylvania on 28 Nov 1940 according to the USS Pennsylvania muster rolls.; He served on the USS Pennsylvania for the duration of the war. He survived the Pearl Harbor attack on 7 December 1941.

Rutherford Revisited, 1996, p. 224 "Another Tri-City boy in service is James Cecil King, 22, son of Mr. and Mrs. Dave King of Rutherford. His is a gunner's mate, 3rd class and has been in the Navy three years. At Pearl Harbor when the Japs attacked he has seen service in the Pacific area since." Article originally published in 1943 *Tri-City Reporter.*

Picture from Wooley/Russell Family Tree on Ancestry.com. Photo originally shared by docwooley1

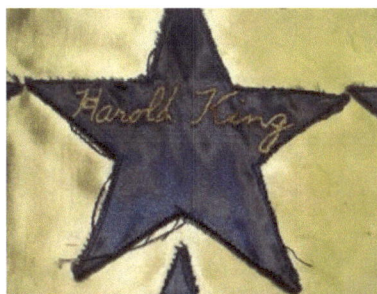

King, Harold [2]- Harold C. King; **Class of 1941** 15 March 1921-5 Nov 2013; son of Clarence and Ollie Hogue King who married 10 October 1909 in Gibson County.; 1930 District 8 Gibson County Census lists Harold, age 9, living with parents Clarence and Ollie; 1940 Rural Gibson Co Census, he is listed with parents; [1982 living in Bartlett, TN according to US Public Records index]; enlisted 19 Nov 1942 with 4 years HS from Gibson Co.; from his obituary: " serving in the 99th Division, of the 924th Field Artillery "

Listed as Harold C King on http://www.fold3.com

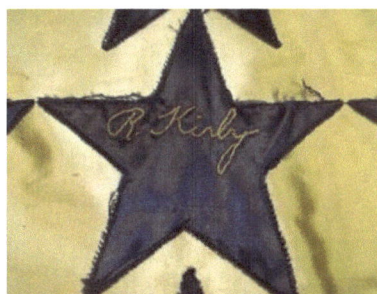

Kirby, R. [11]-Roy Howell Kirby; 3 may 1924-Sept 1982; buried Fairview Cemetery [Find A Grave Memorial# 25683550]; son of Sid Royal and Seicle Darthulia Baumgarder Kirby who married 19 December 1923 in Carroll County, TN; 1930 District 9, Gibson County Census, Roy H. is living with his mother Cecil and her new husband, N.P. Gibbons. (note Sid Royal Kirby died 17 Sept 1925 of Typhoid fever in Carroll County);   military marker; PFC US Army World War II; enlisted 23 Mar 1943 from Dyer Co. with 4 yrs high school
Listed as Roy H Kirby on www.fold3.com

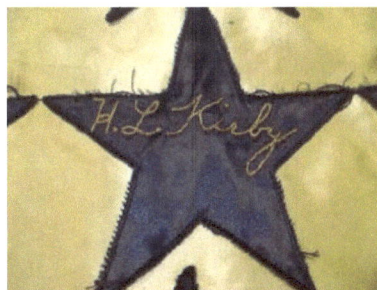

Kirby, H. L. [12]-Horace L. Kirby, Jr.; 20 September 1920-23 Feb 1998, Memphis, TN. ; son of Horace Leslie and Lessie Conly Raville Kirby who were married 7 September 1919 in Crockett County, TN.   1930 District 3, Dyer County census lists H. L. Kirby, age 9, with his parents. (H.L.'s father is a grocery man.)

Kuykendall, H. [14]-James Herbert Kuykendall; **CLASS OF 1937**; 15 Oct 1920-19 Feb 1958; buried in Memphis National Cemetery [Find A Grave Memorial# 3161730]; son of James Newton and Fannie Bell Smith Kuykendall; husband of Frantie Louise Shipp; Navy Muster Rolls list James H. Kuykendall, #934 38 52, as S2c USS Lst 805 16 Dec 1944 with ATB Camp in Norfolk,Va.; later enlistment records show enlistment in the Naval Reserves 10 Feb. 1955 [brother Lloyd Kuykendall served also.] ***Listed on the Veteran's memorial as James Kuykendall**

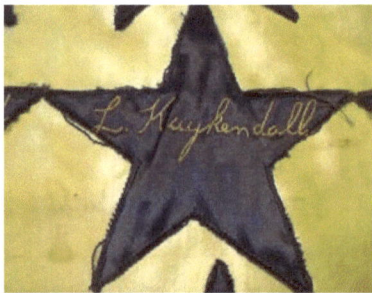

Kuykendall, L. [13]-Lloyd Newton Kuykendall; **CLASS OF 1936**; buried in McCorkle Cemetery in Dyer, Co. [Find A Grave Memorial# 27614586]; son of James Newton and Fannie Bell Smith Kuykendall [brother Herbert Kuykendall served also]; husband of Anna Lois Gregory Kuykendall whom he married in Pensacola, Florida 29 January 1943. Served as a Lieutenant in the Navy during WWII.

His daughters, Kathy and Rose, said that he served as a Navy pilot searching for enemy submarines in the waters around Cuba and South America.
*Listed on the Veteran's Memorial

NOTE: After the war, Lloyd would return to Yorkville High School to teach Agriculture. His bride, Anna Lois, would teach Home Economics.

Wed To Naval Officer

Mrs. Lloyd N. Kuykendall is the former Anna Lois Gregory, daughter of Mr. and Mrs. M. J. Gregory of Dyer, Tenn. Her marriage to Ensign Kuykendall, son of Mr. and Mrs. J. N. Kuykendall of Newbern, Tenn., took place Jan. 29.

Miss Gregory Is Wed To Ensign Kuykendall

Special to The Commercial Appeal

DYER, Tenn., Feb. 20.—Mr. and Mrs. M. J. Gregory of Dyer announce the marriage of their daughter, Anna Lois Gregory, to Ensign Lloyd N. Kuykendall, son of Mr. and Mrs. J. N. Kuykendall of Newbern, Tenn. The wedding took place Jan. 29 at the chapel of the Naval Air Station at Pensacola, Fla., where the bridegroom is an instructor.

The bride attended University of Tennessee Junior College and was graduated from the University of Tennessee where she was a member of Sigma Kappa Sorority. Ensign Kuykendall attended Memphis State College.

The above newspaper clipping announcing the marriage of Lloyd and Anna Lois Gregory Kuykendall was saved in Bettye Loggins' childhood/WWII Era scrap book. The marriage took place 29 January 1943. The newspaper source is unknown.

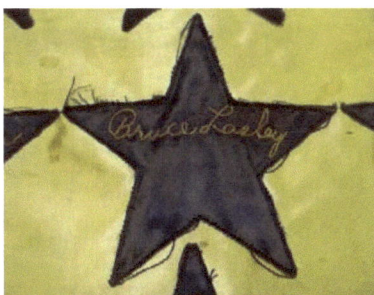

Lasley, Bruce [12]-Gentry Bruce Lasley; 1 Sept 1905-4 May 1984, Eva , Tennessee; buried Chalk Hill Cemetery in Camden, TN [Find A Grave Memorial# 33991374]; son of Frank B. and Sallie Rodgers Travis Lasley who married 27 Feb 1886 in Gibson County; Husband of Louise E. Surratt; enlisted in the Navy 15 December 1941 and served until 28 Jan 1947. He re-enlisted on 16 Jan 1948 and served in the Navy until 8 May 1959.

GENTRY BRUCE LASLEY
YNC US NAVY
WORLD WAR II KOREA
SEP 1 1905   MAY 4 1984

GENTRY BRUCE LASLEY WAS THE OLDEST OF THE YORKVILLE STUDENTS TO SERVE DURING WORLD WAR II.

Legions, K. [12]-Kenneth E. Legions; 1923-1992; buried Memphis Memory Gardens [Find A Grave Memorial# 87047936]; son of George Washington and Opal Kelly Legions with his parents. enlisted 26 Feb 1943 in Army with 2 years High School ***Listed on the Veteran's Memorial**
Listed as Kenneth E. Legions on www.fold3.com

Littleton, F. [1] Franklin Sharp Littleton; born 3 February 1920-2 September 1989; buried Maple Hill Cemetery, Huntsville, Alabama [Find A Grave Memorial# 89262327]; son of Ivie D. and Mattie B. Sharp Littleton who married 16 March 1919 in Gibson County, Tennessee; 1930 District 24 Gibson County Census lists, Frank S Littleton, age 10, living with his paternal grandparents, John F. and Estella Littleton; 1940 Gibson County Census lists Frank Sharp Littleton, age 19 living with his grandparents, John Franklin and Estella Littleton.; enlisted in the Army on 15 February 1942 with 3 years high school; Military Marker: CPL, U.S. Army, World War II.

Yorkville, Tennessee in the 1940's.

Logan, J.R. [10]- John Russell Logan; **CLASS OF 1930/picture**: 17 May 1911-24 February 1988; buried in Yorkville [Find A Grave Memorial# 127627608]; son of Samuel Brown and Mattie Lillie Thomas Hall Logan who married 20 October 1904 in Dyer County; enlisted 3 April 1942 [4 years college] as private; and rose to the rank of Captain. Member of the 1930 Yorkville High School Boys Basket Ball team. ***Listed on the Veteran's Memorial**

Faustina Logan said of John Russell, "He would always asked us about our grades when we would write to him. He was a Captain and Margaret and I thought he was so handsome in his uniform and he really was! Once when he was at home he drove Margaret, Sara Wyatt, Sue Baker, and myself all over Gibson County. We were so turned around that when we got to Rutherford he asked us if we knew where we were and none of us knew! He was always taking pictures of us and would develop them there at his Mother's home." [Margaret is "Tina's" sister. John Russell was their cousin.]

1930 Yorkville Boys Basket Ball Team: Top Row: L.M. Austin; Ed Jones; C.H. Cole, Principal and Coach; John Russell Logan; Middle Row: Theron "Hap" Edmiston; Robert Wade Uselton; Wayne Hendrix; Front Row: Jackson Foster; Clarence Eakes; Douglas Kemp.

Loggins, P. [5]-Phillip Edwards Loggins; **Class of 1939; Vice President:** 12 Feb 1921-28 Nov 1998 in Gainesville, Florida [Find A Grave Memorial# 126735741]; son of Reuben Wilson and Grace Edwards Loggins, Sr. who married 29 November 1917 in Dyer County; [brother, Reuben Wilson Loggins, also in WWII]; 1930 District 8 Gibson County Census lists Reuben, age 11, and Philip, age 9, and baby sister, Bettye Jean, with their parents; Husband of Martha Helen Bell whom he married 14 Feb 1942 in Corinth, MS while on furlough in Gibson County; Enlisted 1939 in Army Air Corp ; 1940 Kendall, Montgomery, Alabama Census lists Philip E. Loggins, abt 1922, as a soldier.[brother, Reuben Wilson Loggins, also in WWII]   Phillip use the GI Bill to earn college degrees. He became a professor of Agriculture at the University of Florida in Gainesville, Tennessee.

*Listed on the Veteran's memorial as Philip Loggins

Phillip's *wife, Martha, outlined his service: "Phillip joined Army Air Corp. out high school in 1939. He wanted to fly but was color blind so he worked on planes and inspected them. He was first stationed at Maxwell Field, Montgomery, Alabama.   He was then transferred to Greenville , Mississippi when we married. [Feb 14, 1942] and then he was sent West Helena, Arkansas [circa 23 April 1943] . His next assignment sent us to Orangeburg, South Carolina. Finally, we were stationed at Columbus, Miss. until end of War."*

DOUBLE WEDDING

Robinson—Enochs
Loggins—Bell

A double wedding of interest to numerous friends in this community was solemnized at Corinth, Miss., last Sunday evening. The contracting parties were Miss Mary Beth Enochs to Mr. Marion Robinson and Miss Martha Bell to Mr. Phillip Loggins. The nuptial knots were tied by the Rev. W. E. Hoyt, pastor of the Cumberland Presbyterian Church at Corinth.

Mrs. Robinson is the former Miss Mary Beth Enochs, daughter of Mr. and Mrs. Joe M Enochs, and is a graduate of the Newbern High School. For the past several months she has been an employe of the Ben Franklin store here. The couple will reside at Milan, where Mr. Robinson is employed at the Wolf Ordnance Plant.

Mrs. Loggins, nee Miss Martha Bell, is the daughter of Mr. and Mrs. Earl Bell and is also a graduate of the Newbern High School. Mr. Loggins at present is in the aviation training school in Greenville, Miss.

While home on furlough, Jack Ramsey and Bob Zarecor, two fellow Yorkville High School graduates who would also be listed on the Yorkville High School Flag, arranged a date for Phillip with Martha Helen Bell on a Saturday night. According to Martha, " we hit it off and he came back on Sunday night and we dated, called and wrote letters until we married."

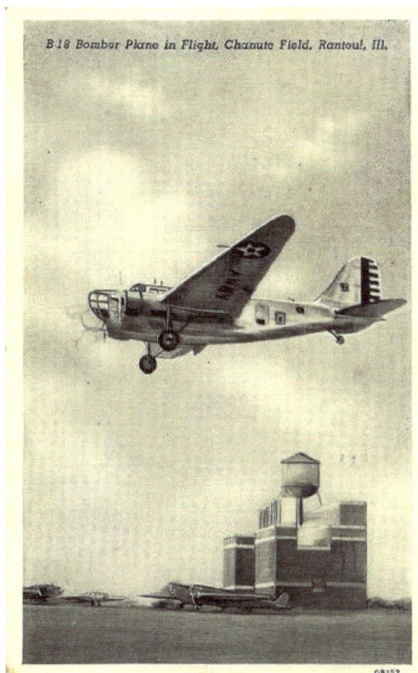

Bettye Jean Loggins stands between her two older brothers, Reuben Wilson Loggins and Phillip Edwards Loggins.

Loggins, R. [6]- Reuben Wilson Loggins, Jr.; **Class of 1938;**

7 Oct 1918-26 August 2000 in Rutherford, TN; buried in the Rutherford Cemetery [Find A Grave Memorial# 97888270] son of Reuben Wilson and Grace Edwards Loggins, Sr. who married 29 November 1917 in Dyer County; 1930 District 8 Gibson County Census lists Reuben, age 11, and Philip, age 9, with their parents; Husband to Dorothy Mildred Reed Loggins whom he married 15 Jan 1942 in Corinth, MS while home in Gibson County on furlough; [brother, Phillip Edwards Loggins in WWII also]; enlisted 28 October 1940 in the Army Air Corps in Washington, D.C.; served in the European Theater and was stationed in England beginning 25 December 1942 ***Listed on the Veteran's Memorial**

Rutherford Revisited, 1996, p. 225 "The promotion of Reuben W. Loggins, Jr. from the grade of Sergeant to Staff-Sergeant was recently announced "Somewhere in England by the Eighth Air Force. He is the husband of Mrs. Dorothy Loggins of Rutherford and a son of Mr. and Mrs. R. W. Loggins of Rutherford, Rt. 1." Originally published in the Tri-City Reporter.

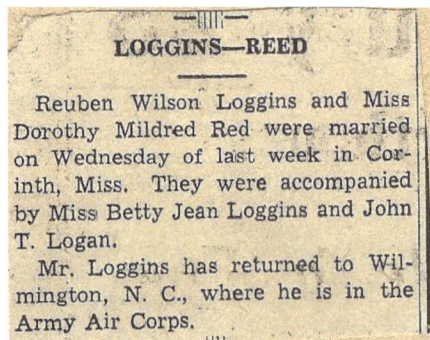

LOGGINS—REED

Reuben Wilson Loggins and Miss Dorothy Mildred Red were married on Wednesday of last week in Corinth, Miss. They were accompanied by Miss Betty Jean Loggins and John T. Logan.

Mr. Loggins has returned to Wilmington, N. C., where he is in the Army Air Corps.

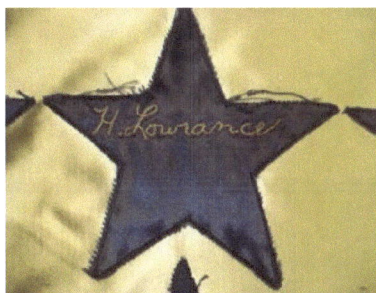

Lowrance, H. [2]-Hollis Lowrance; 30 June 1922-22 January 1990; buried in Yorkville [Find A Grave Memorial# 59170777]; son of Samuel R. and Georgia Lee Morgan Lowrance; He listed as Hollis Lowrance on 1940 Rural Gibson County Census, age 17; husband of Lola Turner of Trenton, Tennessee whom he married 27 December 1943 in Caruthersville, Missouri [Their Pemiscot marriage record states "Three day waiting period waived. Order Probate Judge T.E Broderick." Also both Hollis and Lola use Trenton as their address.] ; enlisted 19 Nov 1942 in Army with 1 year high school

> *Two of his three children, Larry who is a Viet Nam Veteran and Janice told that he was Army and served in the European Theatre. He received a Purple Heart when he was wounded in France in 1944 by a mortar shell that caused damage to his head and shoulder. He served out the rest of the war in England.*

Listed as Hollis F Lowrance on http://www.fold3.com

McDonald, Harold [12} Class of 1943 -Erice Harold McDonald; 30 June 1926 -4 June 2006 Winnsboro, Franklin, Louisiana, Buried in Bells Chapel Cumberland Presbyterian Church Cemetery [Find A Grave Memorial# 32328862]; son of Erice E. and Elizabeth Barkley McDonald who were married 1 July 1917 [*family member related that Erice was home on a furlough during World War I]* in Gibson County ; 1930 District 9 Gibson County Census lists Harold, age 4 9/12 living with his parents; Military Inscription: AKI US Navy; Served aboard: USS Logan, USS Chourre, and USS Alloth

---

Some of the Businesses and Churches in Yorkville "proper" during the 1940's.

Businesses: Boss Parker's Cafe, Pipkin's Grocery Store, Spitzer's Blacksmith, Marvin's Barber Shop, Bank of Yorkville, DX Service Station, Texaco Service Station, Baker's Grocery Store,
Yorkville Telephone Company, Red Ledbetter's Grocery Store, Jesse Pack's Mill, Rostelle Parker's Beauty Shop, Thornton's Cotton Gin, John Wharey's Watch Repair, Gable's Transforming Company
Churches: Bethel Baptist, Yorkville Church of Christ, Yorkville Cumberland Presbyterian.
[List by Bettye Loggins McCaffrey Ellis]

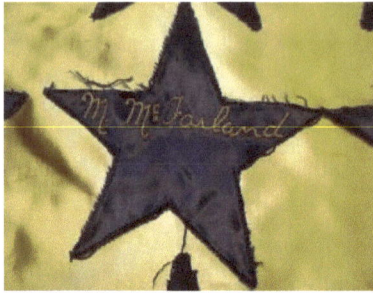

McFarland, M. [2]- Edward Marion McFarland; **Class of 1939**; 12 Feb 1920-17 June 1979; buried in Yorkville [Find A Grave Memorial #25315460]; son of Albert and Edna Robertson McFarland who married 20 April 1919 in Gibson County; 1930 District 8, Dyer County Census lists Marion, age 10, with his parents. 1940 Rural Gibson County census lists Marion, age 20, with his parents. Military Marker: Pfc U.S. Army ***Listed on the Veteran's Memorial as Marion McFarland**

McKnight, Jack [4]- Eugene Jack McKnight; **Class of 1934** 26 Oct 1913-24 Jan 1994 in Newbern; buried in Yorkville [Find A Grave Memorial# 59166421]; husband of Elaine Pierce McKnight whom he married 22 March 1941 in Gibson County; 1941 East Lansing Michigan Directory lists Jack and Elaine.

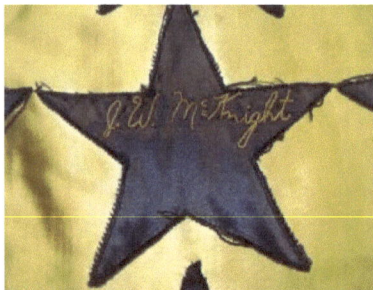

McKnight, J. W. [4]-John William McKnight; 5 June 1919-7 Dec 2000; Buried in the Cool Springs Cumberland Presbyterian Cemetery [Find A Grave Memorial# 57739323] son of Dell Veco and Bradie Mullins McKnight; Enlisted 3 April 1942 with 4 yrs High School.

Letter received by parents: " Leyte, P.I.-- Corporal John W McKnight, son of Mr. and Mrs. Dell V McKnight, Newbern, Tennessee, is homeward bound after   34 months in the Southwest Pacific Area. The Cpl. is being processed for return to the United States at the 28th Replacement Depot (Disposition Center) near Tacloban, Leyte. Corporal McKnight entered the Pacific Theater on Feb. 8, 1943   when he landed at Brisbane, Australia. As a Squad Leader with the headquarters Company of the 2nd Engineers Specialized Brigade he participated in the action around New Guinea, the East Indies and the Philippines. It was the action of his men and himself which won the Presidential Unit Citation when the 2D Engineers Specialized Brigade hit Leyte Island on that eventful 20th day of October 1944.   Transcription by Mary Gay Lewis/ 22 July 2013

Milam, Paul [8]-Paul B Milam, Jr.; Born 5 Oct 1922-30 December 1993 Bay Saint Louis, Mississippi [Find A Grave Memorial# 96241059]; son of Paul B. and Viola Barker Milam who married 31 Dec 1921 in Dyer County; 1930 District 8 Dyer County Census lists Paul Milam, age 8, living with his parents; enlisted 31 Dec 1942 in the Army with 1 year college, married;

Miller, James [7]-James Miller; son of T. Richmond "Dutch" and Annie Lou Parker Miller who were married 5 Aug 1917 in Dyer County ; 1930 District 9 Gibson County Census lists James Miller, age 9, living with his parents. (His father Richmond Miller is the son of T.B. Miller who is buried in the McCorkle Cemetery. Both his mother and father are buried in McCorkle. His uncle, Ollie Miller is buried in Yorkville Cemetery.

Morrow, J. [3]-John Jackson Morrow; 20 Mar 1916-6 Dec. 1995 in Dyersburg.; son of Wade Cleveland and Lillie Leandra Jones Morrow who married 3 Mar 1907 in Madison County. (note: both of his parents are buried in McCullough's Chapel); 1930 District 10 Dyer County Census lists John Morrow, age 14, with his parents; enlisted 9 July 1941 with 2 years high school;

Families anxiously awaited letters from their loved ones in the war. "From Somewhere in England," Wilson Loggins wrote to his mom , "Don't worry about me at all." He then asked about his sister, Bettye, "How much cotton does she pick a day."
30 September 1943

Moyer, Ben [11]-Benjamin Franklin Moyer; 20 October 1924-26 September 2006 Louisville, KY [Find A Grave Memorial# 80801529]; son of Frank Gilbert and Clara Hudson Moore Moyer; 1930 District 9, Dyer County Census lists Bennie, age 6, living with his parents. Enlisted 14 January 1944 in the Army with 3 yrs High School from Gibson county; Discharged 22 September 1945. From his findagrave: " Ben Moyer was a sergeant in the US Army and fought in World War II. He received two medals: The Bronze Star Medal for Meritorious achievement in grand combat against the armed enemy during World War II in the European African Middle Eastern Theater of Operations. The Purple Heart For wounds received in action, Germany 28 November 1944"

Aaron Scott who is the nephew of Frank and Ray Scott related that he and his cousin, Ray, visited with Mr. Moyer after war. Aaron related this story: "Mr. Ben Moyer and my Uncle Ray Scott went to join the Navy on the same day. When they got to the recruiting office, instead of being inducted into the Marines, Roy was inducted into the Marines and Ben into the Army."
Listed as Benjamin F Moyer on www.fold3.com

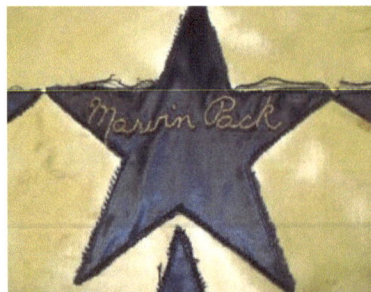

Marvin Pack; **CLASS OF 1940;** 29 Jan 1914-21 Oct 1976; buried in Oakwood Cemetery [Find A Grave Memorial# 15663705]; son of Will Allen and Dora McBride Pack who married 20 December 1906 in Gibson County; enlisted 15 Feb 1942 in the Army with 4 yrs High School and single. His occupation was livestock farmer; Military inscription: Pfc Army World War II.

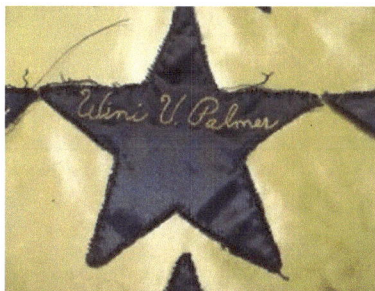

Palmer, Wini V. [11]-Wini V. Palmer; about 1923; daughter of William Egbert and Carrie Estella Webb Palmer; maternal grandparents were Theo and Etta Bradshaw Webb who lived in District 8, Gibson County in the Nebo Community; 1930 District 16 Gibson County census lists Wini V. Palmer, age 7, living with her parents. 1940 Hampton, Lee, Arkansas lists Winnie, age 17, living with her parents. The 1935 notation lists rural Gibson County, Tennessee. Methodist Hospital, Memphis, Tennessee WWII Cadet Nursing Corps records state she entered school 9 September 1941 and entered the Corps 8 March 1943. The record says she graduated from nursing school 4 November 1944.

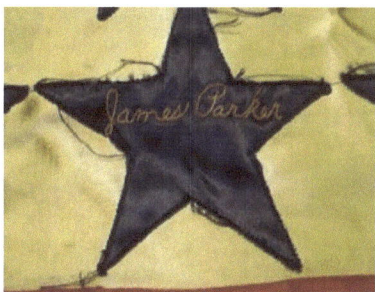

Parker, James [8] -James W. "Jamus" Parker; **Class of 1938/class president;** born 1920; son of James Nathan and Callie Poor Parker who married 2 September 1909 in Dyer County; 1930 Trimble, Dyer County Census lists James W. Parker with his parents.; 1940 Rural Gibson County Census lists Jamus Parker, age 19, living with his parents.; Enlisted 28 September 1942 from Gibson County with 2 years of College;

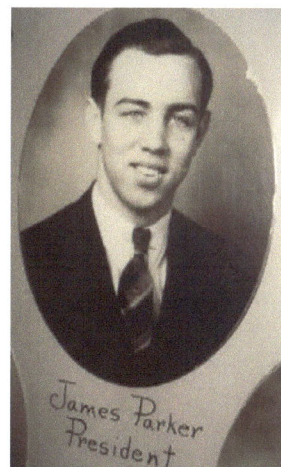

James Parker
President

THE CLASS OF 1936 HAD SEVEN YOUNG MEN TO SERVE IN WORLD WAR II.
WYATT EAKES, GLYN GATES, EMERSON E. JETTON, WILSON JONES,
LLOYD KEYKENDALL, JAMES WESTLEY PARNELL, CARL WILSON SMITH

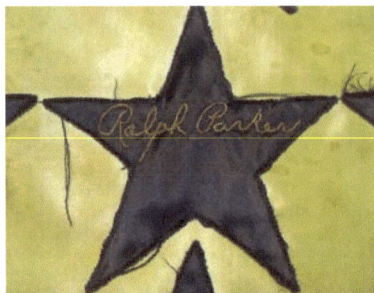

Parker, Ralph [11] Ralph Parker; 22 April 1922- 15 Nov 1993 in Merillville, Indiana; son of Leonard Scobey and Minerva Ann Young Parker who married 17 March 1919 in Dyer County; 1930 District 8 Gibson County Census lists Ralph Parker, age 8, living with his parents; 1940 Rural Gibson county census lists Ralph, age 17, living with his parents.

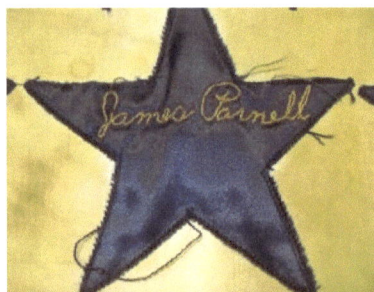

Parnell, James [6] James W. Parnell; **Class of 1936**; born 1917; son of Royal D and Virginia "Virgie" Parnell; 1920 Civil District 21 Gibson County lists James W. age 2 living with his parents; 1930 District 8, Gibson County Census lists James, age 12, living with his parents. 1940 Tipton County Census lists James, age 22, living with his parents with the inferred 1935 Residence as Rural Gibson county; Enlisted 24 May 1941 in the Army as a private with 4 yrs. high school, unmarried, Shelby Co.

James Westley Parnell

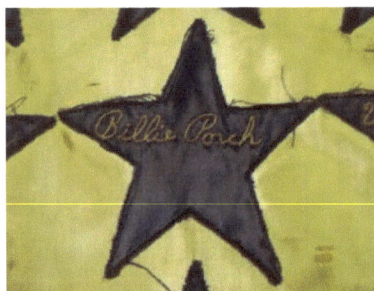

Porch, Billie [13] Billye Porch; 4 June 1923-22 Jan 1993 in Memphis or DeSoto Co, Ms.; son of Boyd and Gussie L. Crenshaw Porch; 1940 Dyer County Census lists Billy Porch, age 15, living with his parents; enlisted 28 June 1944 in the Navy and discharged 13 April 1946

Listed as Billye Porch on Fold3.com

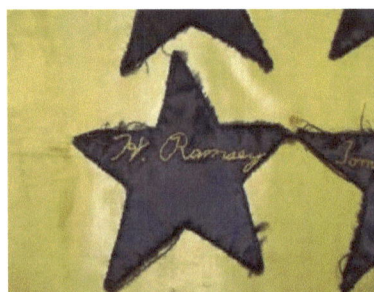

Ramsey, H. [10]-Harlan Bryant Ramsey; 14 May 1927-27 Feb 1949; buried in Mt. Olive Cumberland Presbyterian Cemetery [Find A Grave Memorial# 16028294] ; son of Jeff and Mary Wright Ramsey who married 17 July 1926 in Gibson County; Military Marker: S1 USNR World War II.; Served aboard the USS New Jersey and the USS Charles S Sperry

Ramsey, Jack [3]- Robert Jackson Ramsey; **Class of 1938;** 6 Sept 1920 in Ardmore, Carter County Oklahoma-still living on 4 May 2014; son of Robert E. and Myrtle Ramsey; [His parents are listed on the 1 January 1920 Ardmore, Ward 1, Carter County, Oklahoma Census. His father is a clothing store salesman.] 1930 District 8 Gibson County Census lists Jack with his parents and siblings. Enlisted in the Army 24 July 1943 with the following skills: Skilled linemen and servicemen, telegraph, telephone, and power

Listed on the Veteran's Memorial

Mr. Jack Ramsey said, " I served in the European Theatre with the Third Army. I ended up in Aachen, Germany."

Jack points to his star on the World War II Banner at the dedication held on May 4, 2014.

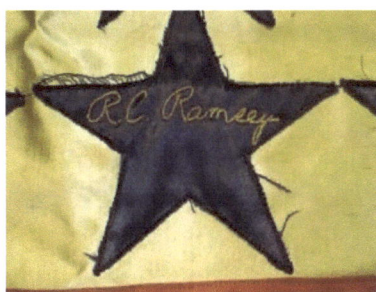

Ramsey, R. C. [9]- Robert C. "R. C." 25 Nov 1921-3 April 2003 **CLASS OF 1942;** buried Spring Hill Cemetery, Nashville, TN [Find A Grave Memorial# 127738428]son of Robert "Bob" and Mary D. Cummings Ramsey who married in 1921 in Gibson County; 1930 District 8 Gibson County Census lists Robert, age 8, with his parents; 1940 Rural Gibson County Census lists R.C., age 18, with his parents; Enlisted in the Navy; rank at discharge: Petty Officer 1st Class

Robert C. Ramsey, Coxswain in Navy, has been discharged from service after 42 months service. He spent 14 months on Pacific duty, where he took part in two invasions and two major engagements. He is the son of Mr. and Mrs. Bob Ramsey of Dyer.

31 Jan 1946 TRI-CITY REPORTER

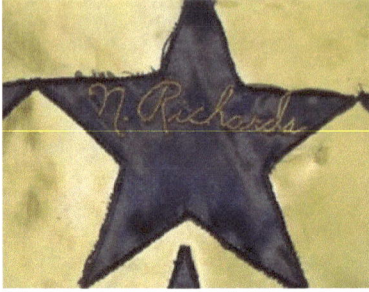

Richards, N. [5]-Neely Thomas Richards; 6 April 1925-10 February 2008; buried Bells Chapel [Find A Grave Memorial# 59396112] son of Willie Lee and Jimmie Maude Reed Richards who married 29 June 1917; 1930 District 8 Gibson County census lists, Gerald F., age 9, and Neely T. , age 5, living with their parents who are in the household of his maternal grandparents, James M. and Alice Reed.; Enlisted in the Navy on 30 March 1943; served aboard USS Suwanne (CVE 27) and USS Munda   Brothers Neely and Gerald both served.

*Listed on the Veteran's Memorial

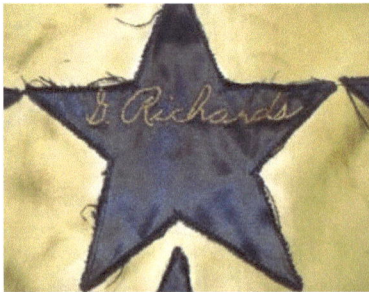

Richards, G. [6]-Gerald Fay Richards; 1 Oct 1920-16 Sept 1958; buried in Bells Chapel [Find A Grave Memorial# 59396217]; son of Willie Lee and Jimmie Maude Reed Richards who married 29 June 1917; 1930 District 8 Gibson County census lists, Gerald F., age 9, and Neely T. , age 5, living with their parents who are in the household of his maternal grandparents, James M. and Alice Reed.; enlisted 27 Aug 1942 in Army; [Brother Neely Richards in WWII also] ***Listed on the Veteran's Memorial**

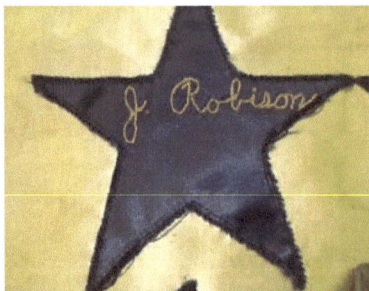

Robison, J. [10] Jack Wright Robison; **Class of 1944;** 2 November 1925-still living on 4 May 2014; son of Jack and Mildred Robison who married 9 June 1917 in Lake County; 1930 Memphis, Shelby County Census lists James R. and Jack V. Robison with their parents; 1940 Gibson county census lists James R, age 19, and Jack, age 14, living with their parents; Served in the United States Navy aboard the USS Charles J. Kimmel (DE-584) that sailed from the Leyte Gulf on 14 September 1945.

[Robbie McCutchen, a cousin-in-law to Jack Wright and James Robert Robison, was helpful in the research of these two men.]

1944 Yorkville High School Basketball Teams

YORKVILLE

Boys		Girls	
Bobbie Baker		Peggy Baker	11
Lindle Cardwell	9	Helen Childress	4
Everette Carroll	3	Kathryn Collins	10
Robert Heathcock	8	Nerine Collins	Alt.
John T. Logan	1	Christine Gabel	Alt.
Thomas McCutchen	Alt	Catherine Lasley	7
Buford Parnell	Alt.	Wilma Sue Legions	3
Billie Gene Ramsey	4	Mildred Morris	6
Jack Robeson	5	Virginia Pope	8
Hal Robeson	2	Linda Fay Ramsey	9
		Dorothy Wyatt	Alt.
Coach: J. L. Doran		Coach: J. L. Doran	

Jack Robison, spelled with an e on this vintage schedule, is listed as one of the 1944 Basketball team. Everette Carroll is listed, too.

John T. Logan who is listed on the 1944 Basketball schedule was seriously wounded on Thanksgiving Day, November 30, 1944 when the shot gun with which he had been hunting accidentally went off. The doctors from the World War II B-17 Training Base in Halls, Tennessee were called in on the case. Inspired by the military doctors, John T. shared with his cousin, Sonny Farrar, that he was going to join the Army Air Force when he got better. Sadly, even with the antibiotics that were available to the Army Air Force, John T. passed away on December 6, 1944 in the Dyersburg Hospital.

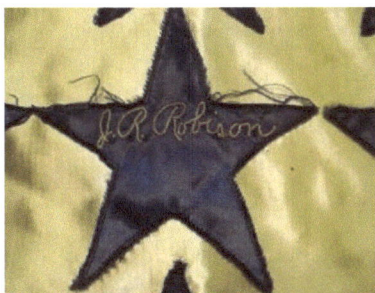

Robison, J.R. [3]-James Robert Robison; born about 1920; Known as "Cotton" in Yorkville; son of Jack and Mildred Robison who married 9 June 1917 in Lake County; 1930 Memphis, Shelby County Census lists James R. and Jack V. Robison with their parents; 1940 Gibson county census lists James R, age 19, and Jack, age 14, living with their parents (note: The family is living near to the household of Charlie and Adiola Cowan); James R. is a mechanic in his father's garage in 1940.

A number of the young men who are listed on the Yorkville World War II Service Flag were from the near by community of Neboville. Once students completed the 8th grade at the Nebo school they began their high school careers at Yorkville High School. *Thanks to Ray Scott for providing this 1940 picture of the Nebo School.*

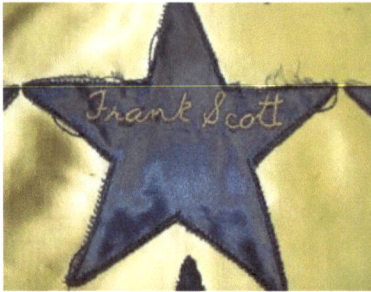

Scott, Frank [2]-Franklin Taylor Scott; **CLASS OF 1941**; born 28 March 1921-10 Feb 2006 Yazoo City, MS; buried in Yorkville [Find A Grave Memorial# 107496776] ; son of Lemuel Locke and Eula Wimberly Scott who married 24 August 1902 in Gibson County; 1940 Gibson County Census lists Frank, age 19, and Ray, age 15 , living with their parents Lemmie and Eula; [Brother to Wilson Ray Scott]

US Army Service **Record from Frank's Honorable Discharge papers includes the following information: Inducted 19 Nov 1942 and entered into active service 27 Nov 1942. Radio Operator Low Speed 776/Combat Infantryman badge. Served 11 months, 15 days in European Theatre in Rhineland; Central Europe/ He departed for ETO on 3 Feb 1945./Served with HQ CO 3rd BN 318th INF REGT./ Wounded in Germany April 1945. Received: American Theater Ribbon, EAME Theater Ribbon W/2 Bronze Stars; Good Conduct Ribbon; Purple Heart; Victory Medal. He was 6 feet tall and 170 lbs. with blue eyes and brown hair. A bench dedicated in memory of Frank and Wilson Ray Scott is part of the Veteran's memorial in the Yorkville Cemetery. *Listed on the Veteran's Memorial**

His nephew, Ray Scott, shared that his uncle was wounded in Germany and captured by the Germans He was a POW for about two weeks before the war with Germany ended . Many thanks to his daughters, Gail Young and Cindy King, for the picture and papers.

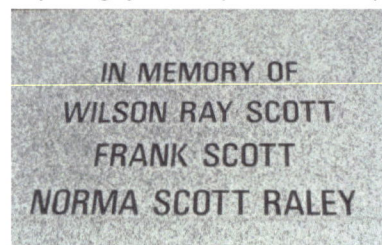

IN MEMORY OF
WILSON RAY SCOTT
FRANK SCOTT
NORMA SCOTT RALEY

A bench in memory of Frank and his brother, Wilson Ray Scott, are a part of the Yorkville Cemetery's Veteran's Memorial.

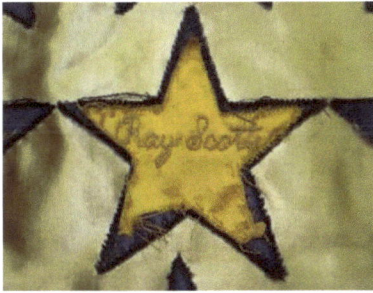

Scott, Ray (Gold Star) [4]-Wilson Ray Scott; 10 October 1924-4 December 1944 Saipan Island, Marianas Islands; **buried in Yorkville** [Find A Grave Memorial #127559290] son of Lemuel Locke and Eula Wimberly Scott who married 24 August 1902 in Gibson County; 1940 Gibson County Census lists Frank, age 19, and Ray, age 15 , living with their parents Lemmie and Eula; [Brother to Franklin Taylor Scott] Military Information: Pvt in Co. G. 2nd BN 6th Marines

Lemuel Scott, father of Ray Wilson Scott, received a penciled note giving minimum information about Ray's death from Ray's commanding officer. The family learned later, according to Aaron and Ray Scott, that their uncle had died trying to save a fellow shipmate from drowning. [Note: By plane, Saipan is about 45 minutes from Guam, 3 hours from Japan, 4 hours from the Philippines. According to http://www.6thmarines.marines.mil/About/History.aspx, the 2nd Marine Division of the 6th Marine Regiment participated in the following actions during the later part of 1944 (Ray's enlistment date was circa 14 Nov. 1944.): "**25 May 1944-**6th Marines departed Pearl Harbor enroute [sic] to Saipan in the Marianas; **15 June - 10 July 1944-**6th Marines participated in the battle for Saipan; **24 July - 1 August 1944-**6th Marines participated in the battle for Tinian.]"

(Left) "*To Lem Scott: Deeply regret to inform you that your son Pfc Wilson R. Scott, USMC, drowned on Dec 4th 1944 at Saipan Island. When information is received regarding burial you will be informed. To prevent possible aid to our enemy Do not divulge the name of his ship or station.*
Please accept my heart felt sympathy.
A.A. Vanderdrife [difficult to read] Letter will follow.

Aaron Scott, who is the nephew of Frank and Ray Scott, related that he and his cousin, Ray Scott, visited with Mr. **Ben Moyer,** who is listed on the Yorkville World War II Service Flag, after the war. Aaron related this story: "Mr. Ben Moyer and my Uncle **Ray Scott** went to join the Navy on the same day. [Ben Moyer's enlistment in the Army is given as 14 January 1944.] When they got to the recruiting office, instead of being inducted into the Marines, Ben was inducted into the Army and Ray was inducted into the Marines."

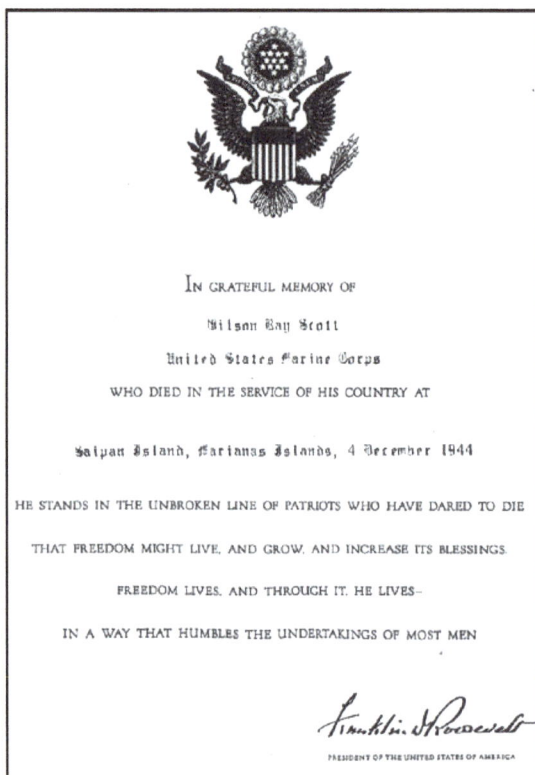

In grateful memory of

Wilson Ray Scott

United States Marine Corps

WHO DIED IN THE SERVICE OF HIS COUNTRY AT

Saipan Island, Marianas Islands, 4 December 1944

HE STANDS IN THE UNBROKEN LINE OF PATRIOTS WHO HAVE DARED TO DIE

THAT FREEDOM MIGHT LIVE, AND GROW, AND INCREASE ITS BLESSINGS.

FREEDOM LIVES, AND THROUGH IT, HE LIVES—

IN A WAY THAT HUMBLES THE UNDERTAKINGS OF MOST MEN

Franklin D Roosevelt

PRESIDENT OF THE UNITED STATES OF AMERICA

**Wilson Ray Scott is listed on the Special section of the Yorkville Cemetery Veteran's Memorial for those who made the supreme sacrifice. In addition a bench dedicated the memory of Frank and Ray Scott is a part of the Veteran's memorial in the Yorkville Cemetery.

ALL GAVE SOME - THESE GAVE ALL
WILLSON RAY SCOTT   KENNETH MARTIN
DAVID EDMISTON   BOBBY J. LEMONS

On June 30, 2014, Ray and Aaron Scott shared the family's framed military picture of Wilson Ray Scott during the Neboville Methodist Church Patriotic Service. According to a list compiled by Thelma F. Scott, Janie F. Putman, and Sylvia F. Moore, USMC Wilson Ray Scott was among the 50 young men from the Neboville Church who served during World War II. In addition to Wilson Ray Scott, the following Neboville Methodist Church boys are listed on the Yorkville WWII Service Flag: Dennis Carlton, Robert Clark, Freeman Dodson, Junior Dunnigan, Guy Hall, James Hall, Robert Harrell, Jamie Jackson, Emerson Jetton, Harold Kin, Kenneth Legion, Billy Porch, Carl Smith

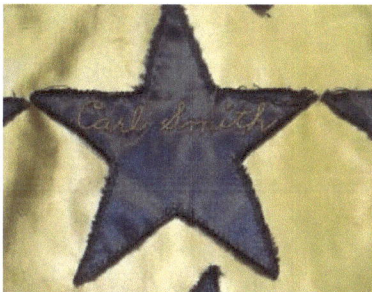

Smith, Carl [4] -Carl Wilson Smith **CLASS OF 1936;** 1 Jan 1918-April 28, 2004 in Trenton; buried in Sunnyside Cemetery; [Find A Grave Memorial# 27712043]son of William Benard and Florence Bell Shaw Smith who were married 18 November 1916 in Gibson County; 1920 District 8 Census lists Carl Wilson, age 2, with his parents Willie Benard and Florence Bell Smith; 1930 District 8 Gibson county Census lists Carl W. Smith, age 12, as the only child with his parents, Bill and Florence; husband of Vera Marie "June" Spence Smith ; 1940 Rural Gibson County Census lists Carl W. Smith with wife, June Smith; Military Marker inscription: TEC 4 US ARMY WORLD WAR II; ***Listed on the Veteran's Memorial**

Listed as Car W Smith 1918 Shelby County on www.fold3.com

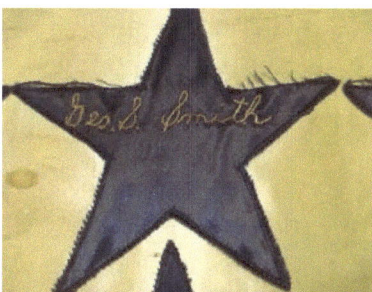

Smith, Geo. S. [10]- George Scott Smith; 1 Dec 1916-30 June 1990; buried Fairview Cemetery in Dyersburg [Find A Grave Memorial# 49054895]; son of George Munsey and Gladys Headden Smith who married 18 Dec 1913 in Dyer county and are buried in Mt. Carmel Methodist Chruch Cemetery; 1920 District 9, Gibson County Census lists George Scott Smith, age 3 1/2, living with his parents; 1930 District 9 Dyer County Census lists George S Smith, age 13, living with his parents.; Military Marker: TEC 3 in US Army WWII.

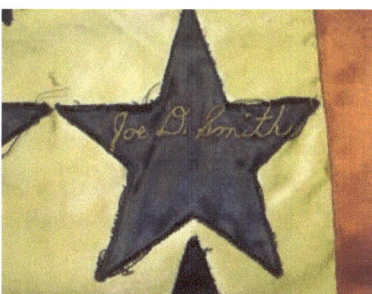

Smith, Joe D. [14]-Joe D. Smith; Born 1923; son of Jim and May Smith; 1930 District 8 Gibson County Census lists Joe D. Smith with parents and siblings: Claudie (11), James (8); Enlisted 30 March 1943 in Army as a private with a grammar school education. **Listed on the Veteran's Memorial**

Danny Jackson, who was an important part of the committee to establish a Veteran's Memorial in the Yorkville Cemetery, shared that Joe D. Smith was with the Big Red One in Italy. [note: 1st Infantry division of the United States Army.]
Listed as Joe D Smith 1923 Gibson County on www.fold3.com

Smith, V. [13]-*can't find* A Vernon Smith is on the Neboville Methodist Church list of the young men who served from that congregation during World War II.

Summers, B. [10] Billie Summers **CLASS OF 1943 , Vice President of his class;** son of Otis and Ruth Couch Summers who married 8 Jan 1927 in Dyer Co.; 1930 District 8 Gibson County Census, Billie is 4 living with his parents.; 1940 Rural Gibson County Census has Billie living with his parents and a younger sister, Patsy Joe.

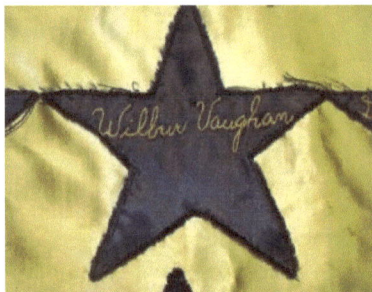

Vaughan, Wilbur [3] - James Wilbur Vaughn; **CLASS OF 1935;** 21 March 1917- 13 April 1996 Martin, TN [Find A Grave Memorial# 55765177]; son of son of James Bone and Anna Bell Phillips Vaughn who married 6 Oct 1915 ; 1930 District 8 Gibson County Census lists James, age 13, living with his parents. 1940 Gibson County Census lists Wilbur, age 22, living with his parents.

*Listed on the Veteran's Memorial

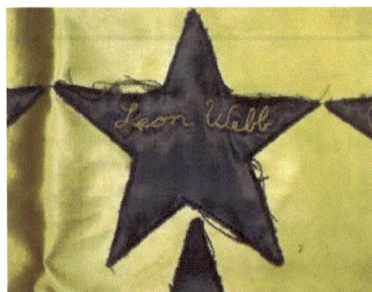

Webb, Leon [9]-Robert Leon Webb; 16 Oct 1922-26 Nov 1969 buried in Oakwood [Find A Grave Memorial# 15680434]; son of Clyde and Hattie Lou McFarland Webb who married 12 February 1921 in Dyer County; 1930 District 8 Dyer County Census lists Robert Lee [sic], age 8, with his parents; 1940 Rural Gibson County Census lists Leon, age 17, living with parents in his 3rd year of High School; Enlisted 24 December 1942 from Gibson County with 3 yrs HS; Inscription on military marker: Tennessee Tec 5 HQ 238 Engr Combat Bn World War II ;

Listed as Robert L Webb born 1922 on www.fold3.com

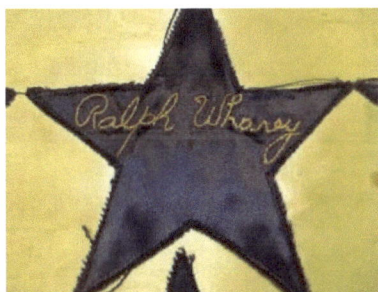

Wharey, Ralph [9]- Ralph H. Wharey; **CLASS OF 1940;** 3 Oct 1920- 21 November 2000; buried in Memphis Funeral Home and Memorial Gardens [Find A Grave Memorial# 76700420] son of

John Lipscomb and Eula McCage Wharey.; 1930 District 8 Gibson County census lists Ralph, age 9, with his parents; 1940 8th Civil District, Yorkville census lists Ralph, age 19, living with his parents. [His father, Mr. John Wharey is serving as Justice of the Peace.] enlisted 25 October 1942 in Army with 4 yrs High School from Gibson County; 21 March 1946 TRI-CITY REPORTER: "Ralph Wharey is at home after spending several months overseas."
www.fold3.com lists him as Ralph H. Wharey Birth 1920 Alabama but neither the 1930 District 8 Gibson county nor the 1940 Gibson County Censuses list a birth place other than Tennessee.]

Whitley, Glen[4] -**CLASS OF 1931 /picture;** Harrison Glen Whitley; 10 Feb 1911- 10 Dec 1989 Memphis, Tennessee; son of John W. and Cora L. Grisham Whitley of the Bells Chapel Community; 1920 District 8 Gibson Co census lists Glen, age 8, living with his parents and born about 1912.; 1930 District 8 Gibson County Census lists Harrison G., age 19 living with his parents; Enlisted 10 March 1942 in the Army with 4 years high school from Gibson County.

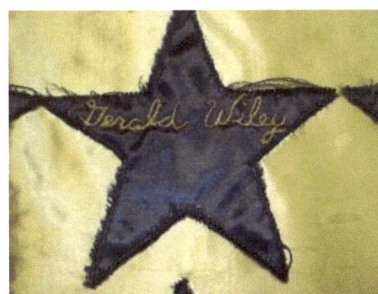

Wiley, Gerald [4]- Gerald C. Wiley, Jr.; 16 January 1926 - 16 October 2001 in Memphis [Find A Grave Memorial# 78768790]son of Gerald C. Wiley, Sr., and Kittie Alma Peevyhouse Wiley, who married 11 August 1915 in Gibson County; 1930 District 8 Gibson County Census lists Raymond, age 11, and Gerald, age 6, living with their parents.; 1940 Rural Gibson County census lists Gerald, age 14, living with his parents; His obituary states that he was a Navy Veteran. Brother to Raymond Wiley who was in WWII also.

Wiley, Raymon [10] Raymond L Wiley; 17 September 1918-22 Jan 1992buried in Yorkville [Find A Grave Memorial# 19507878]; ; son of Gerald C. and Kittie Alma Peevyhouse, Sr., who married 11 August 1915 in Gibson County, Tennessee; 1920 District 8 Gibson County census lists Raymond Wiley, age 1 2/12, living with his parents. 1930 District 8 Gibson County Census lists Raymond, age 11, and Gerald, age 6, living with their parents.; Husband of Lucille Johnston Wiley whom he married 8 April 1939; Enlisted 22 April 1944 as a private, married, 2 years high school from Gibson County.; Military Marker: S SGT US Army ***Listed on the Veteran's Memorial**; Brother to Gerald Wiley who was in WWII also.

WITH TRI-CITY BOYS IN SERVICE

EIGHTH ARMY HEADQUARTERS, YOKOHAMA, JAPAN—Technician Fifth Grade (Corporal) Raymond L. Wiley, son of Mrs. G. C. Wiley, Yorkville, Tenn., has been promoted to the rank of Staff Sergeant by the 387th Infantry Regiment, now occupying Gumma Prefecture, Japan.

During the war in Europe, Sga. Wiley saw action, as a member of the 387th, in the Ruhr Pocket and Czechoslovakian Campaigns. He holds several military ribbons and decorations, including the Combat Infantryman's Badge.

Following the surrender of Germany, he returned to the United States, spent a 30-day recuperation leave with his wife and mother, then sailed for the Orient with Major General H. F. Kramer's 97th Infantry Division—the first veteran ETO combat division to land on the Japanese homeland.

10 January 1946
TRI CITY REPORTER

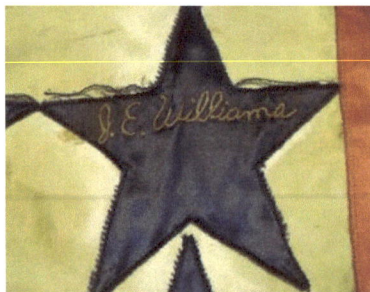

Williams, J. E. [14]-James Edward "Jim" Williams; **Class of 1935;** 24 December 1917- 9 November 2010 in Dallas, Texas; son of Albert Leroy and Vera Louise Edwards Williams who married 29 Nov 1914 in Dyer County; 1920, District 8 Gibson County Census lists him as James Edward, age 2 2/12, living with his parents.; 1930 District 8 Gibson County Census lists him as James, age 12, living with his parents. Enlisted 2 April 1941 in Shelby County with 4 years HS and married

James Edward Williams

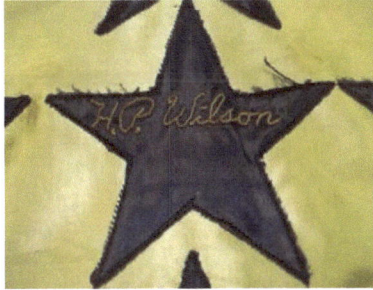

Wilson, H. P. [10]- Harry Parks Wilson; **Class of 1937;** 21 November 1918-May 26 1978; buried in the Rutherford Cemetery [Find A Grave Memorial# 27509521]; son of Thomas Lester and Ruby Elizabeth Cowan Wilson who married 8 Feb 1918 in Gibson county; 1920 District 8 Gibson County Census lists Harry Parks, age 1 3/12, living with his parents.; 1930 District 8 Gibson County Census lists Harry P. living with his parents.; Enlisted 6 Dec 1939 in the Navy; Service #295 53 95) Served aboard USS Pinola (ATO-33) and USS Helios (ARB -12)Discharged as a BM 1 US Navy WWII

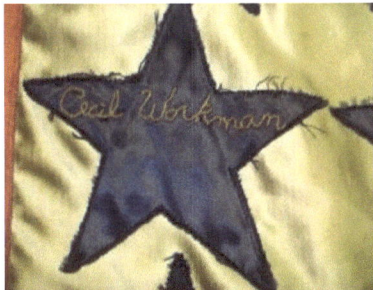

Workman, Cecil [1] Cecil D. Workman; **Class of 1940 as class president;** 1919-; son of James Thomas and Ollie B Hill Workman who married 18 December 1910 in Gibson county; 1930 Rutherford, Gibson County Census lists Cecil D, age 9, living with his parents ; 1940 Rural Gibson Co Census taken on 1 April 1940. lists Cecil, age 20, with his parents and completed a 3 year HS level of education.; enlisted 3 April 1941 as a private in the Army from Gibson County; Listed as Cecil D Workman on www.Fold3.com

During the Senior Year of the class of 1938, Japan invaded China on July 7, 1937 and Hitler annexed Austria on March 12, 1938. The quiet community of Yorkville that this picture from the 1938 YHS Graduation Composite shows seemed to be faraway from the troubled world.

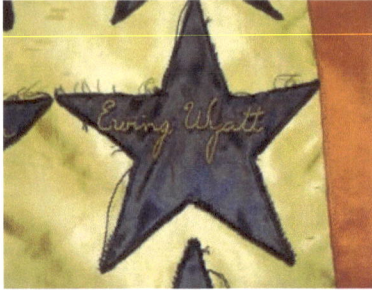

Wyatt, Ewing [14]-Finis Ewing Wyatt, Jr.; [**composite picture unavailable**, picture from 1921-22 Music Class] 24 July 1909-17 May 1995; son of Dr. Finis Ewing and Ora Blanche Turner Wyatt who married 25 Oct 1899 in Gibson County; 1910 District 8 Gibson County Census lists Finis E. Wyatt, Jr. , age 8/12, living with his parents; 1930 Martin, Weakley County Census lists Ewing Wyatt, age 20, as a student living with his widowed mother; enlisted 28 July 1942 in Army with 3 years college; Listed as Finis E Wyatt on http://www.fold3.com ***Listed on the Veteran's Memorial**

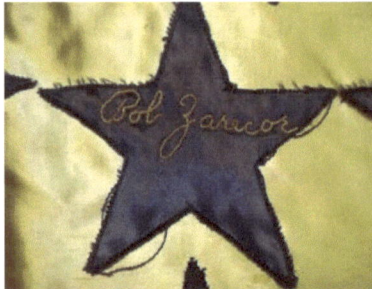

Zarecor, Bob [2]-Robert Allen Zarecor, Jr.; **Class of 1939** 28 May 1919-8 June 2009; buried in Yorkville [Find a grave #38195290]; son of Robert Allen and Amma Pope Zarecor who married 18 Feb 1911. 1940 Gibson county Census lists Robert A., age 21, with father and mother and brother, G. Oppie (Jack), age 18, and sister, Sara, age 15. [Sara helped sew the flag]. Enlisted 9 July 1941 in Army; Pfc AT 254 Infantry; Included in 63rd Infantry Division History ***Listed on the Veteran's Memorial and a bench that is part of the Veteran's Memorial**

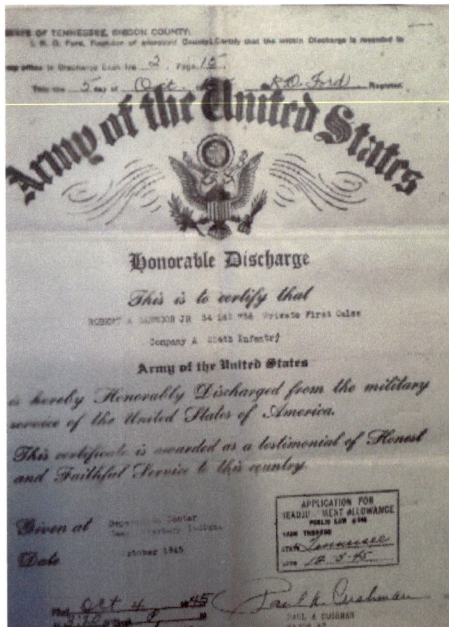

[Family Story: Bob enlisted in July for a 12 month service time before the Pearl Harbor Bombing. His 12 months turned into 52 months.]

THE CREATOR OF THE WORLD WAR II YHS SERVICE FLAG

Mrs. Alline Harris Taylor (1919-1980) was the only child of Sidney S. "Sid" and Birdie Hale Harris who married 3 March 1905 in Gibson County. In the 1910 District 8 Gibson County Census, Alline is listed as 1 2/12 living with her parents. In the 1920 District 8 Gibson County Census, Alline, age 10, is listed with her parents.; According to the 1927 graduation program for Yorkville High School, Alline Harris was in the Class of 1927. In the 1930 Lest We Forget annual for Union University, Alline Harris, Yorkville is listed in the Junior Class. (note: Estelle McCutcheon of Yorkville is also in this class.) Alline married Robert J. Taylor on 28 June 1933. (Rev. N.M. Stigler performed the ceremony.) In the 1940 Gibson County Census, Alline and Robert J. are living with her parents. Both are listed as teachers with 4 years of college. Alline's last year to teach Home Economics at Yorkville was 1944. She was pregnant at the time with her first child. Alline and Robert are listed in the 1947 Mobile, Alabama Directory. Alline and Robert J. are buried in the Yorkville Cemetery. [Her Find A Grave Memorial# 19508070]

The Service Flag now hangs in the Yorkville Community Center. This picture was made 15 August 2014 at the Annual Fish Fry that takes place during Yorkville's International Washer Pitchin' Contest that is held the 3rd week end in August, which was the same time that the Yorkville Jersey Cattle Show was held.

THE HOME EC "GIRLS"--THE CLASSES OF 1943 AND 1944

On May 25, 1994, Marion Jetton Stewart wrote to her fellow Class of 1946 classmates, "Do you remember the Home Ec girls sewing the 'Service Flag'?"
We know for certain that Janie Hundley and Katherine Collins worked on the flag because they sent messages to Bettye Jean Loggins McCaffrey Ellis. There are no records of the others. [Note: The center 37 stars were added by later Home Ec girls.]

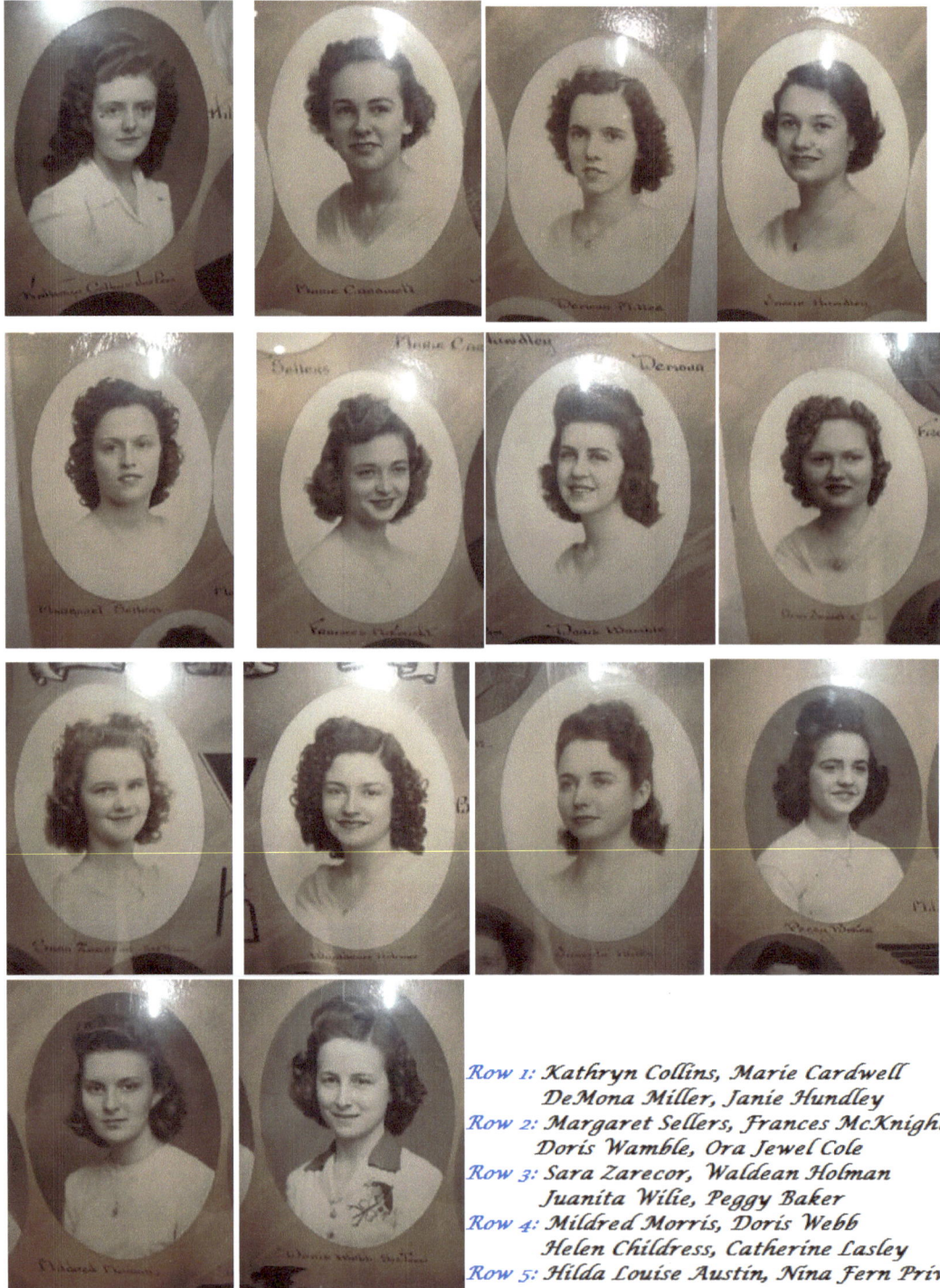

Row 1: Kathryn Collins, Marie Cardwell
DeMona Miller, Janie Hundley
Row 2: Margaret Sellers, Frances McKnight
Doris Wamble, Ora Jewel Cole
Row 3: Sara Zarecor, Waldean Holman
Juanita Wilie, Peggy Baker
Row 4: Mildred Morris, Doris Webb
Helen Childress, Catherine Lasley
Row 5: Hilda Louise Austin, Nina Fern Privette

The following family members of some of the young men whose names were on the Service Flag were there for the dedication of the newly framed flag on May 2, 2014 at the Yorkville Community Center.

Jamie Jackson's son, Danny

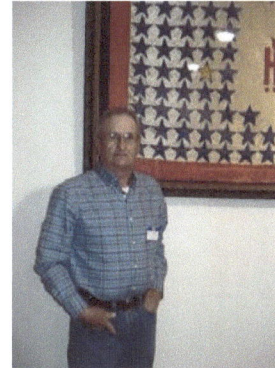

Frank and Wilson Ray Scott's nephews: Aaron and Ray

The daughters of Llyod Kuykendall and the nieces of James Hurbert Kuykendall: Kathy and Roseanne

Hollis Lowrance's Children: Janice and Larry

Bob Zarecor's children: Barbara and Mack

THE RESEARCH COMPILER AND HER SOURCES

Gwendolyn "Gwen" McCaffrey McReynolds
I am the niece of Reuben Wilson and Phillip Edwards Loggins. I compiled this information in April, May, June, July, September, and October of 2014 using the records on Ancestry.com, Find a Grave.com, Fold3.com, *Tri-City Reporter*, and Google sources as well as input from Bettye Loggins McCaffrey Ellis, who is the sister of Wilson and Phillip and who spent from 1929-1953 and from 1969 until the current time in Yorkville and was the Yorkville field office secretary for U.S. Congressman Ed Jones, brother to Wilson Jones. Dorothy Mildred Reed Loggins, who is the wife of Wilson and a life long resident of Gibson county was also a consultant. Barbara Zarecor Turner, who is the daughter of Bob Zarecor and a resident of Yorkville since birth, also assisted. In addition, my mother and I visited the Veterans' Memorial at the Yorkville Cemetery and viewed and photographed the Yorkville High School composite pictures for Classes 1930-1944 that are housed in the Yorkville Community Center to find the names of the men listed on the Banner. Sharon Farrar Krieger, daughter of Bill Farrar and niece of H.L. Farrar, provided the 1927 Yorkville High School Commencement program. Sonny Farrar, son of H. L. Farrar and cousin to Bettye and Gwen, provided the graduation information for his father and supplied the 1929 YHS composite pictures. In addition, Mother and I collected information while attending the May 2, 2014 Service Flag Dedication, the June 30, 2014 Patriotic Program at the Neboville Methodist Church, and the August 15, 2014 International Washer Pitchin' Contest Fish Fry. Members of LIFE IN YORKVILLE Facebook site also provided information and numerous other members of the Veteran's Families and Yorkville residents. I have noted sources in the entries.

[Above Picture: On 2 May 2014 at the dedication of the newly framed Service Flag, Wilson and Phillip's sister, Bettye, and their niece, Gwen, pose with H. L. Farrar's son and Bill Farrar's nephew, Henry "Sonny". Bettye is also first cousin to H.L. and Bill Farrar.]

63

LEGEND

Row 1 Down: Crowder, R.**;** Littleton, F.**;** Culp, Ted**;** **Jetton, J.L.;** Workman, Cecil**;** Agnew, B. **;** Gabel, Joe L.**;** Boucher, L. **;** Black, William**;** Forrester, D.

Row 2 Down: Lowrance, H.**;** Scott, Frank**;**McFarland, M.**;** Dodson, F.**;** Zarecor, Bob**;** Eakes, H. M**;** Johnson, J.**;** Cardwell, J.C.**;** King, Harold**;** Allmon, E.

Row 3 Down: Brown, Verlon**;** Morrow, J.**;** Robinson, J.R.**;** Collins, J.L.**;** Vaughan, Wilbur**;** Ramsey, Jack**;** Flatt, W.**;** Kilpatrick, B.**;** Childress, M.**;** Jackson, Logan

Row 4 Down: Edmiston, R. F. (Gold Star)**;** McKnight, J. W. **;** Brown, J. T.**;** McKnight, Jack**;** Wiley, Gerald**;** Scott, Ray (Gold Star)**;** Smith, Carl**;** Jetton, E.E.**;** Whitley, G.**;** Bernard, F. M.

Row 5 Down: Edmiston, E.E.**;** Granthan, R. A.**;** Austin, K.**;** Crouse, J. T.**;** Carrol, L.**;** Galloway, J.**;** Bradford, L.**;** Harrell, Robert**;** Richards, N.**;** Loggins, P.

Row 6 Down: Edmiston, T.**;** Parnell, James**;** Carrell, E**;** Richards, G.**;** Loggins, R.

Row 7 Down: Gates, G.L.**;** Jones, W. (gold star)**;** Miller, James**;** Dunagan, Jr.

Row 8 Down: Halford, R.**;** Milam, Paul**;** Austin, F.**;** Parker, James

Row 9 Down: Wharey, Ralph**;** Fowlkes, M.**;** Davis, C. **;** Webb, Leon**;** Ramsey, R. C.

Row 10 Down: Smith, Geo. S.**;** Wilson, H. P.**;** Summars, B.**;** Ramsey, H.**;** Cardwell, G. Black, Seagle**;** Robinson, J.**;** Wiley, Raymon**;** Halford, C.**;** Logan, J.R.

Row 11 Down: King, C.**;** Kirby, R.**;** Henderson, J.L.**;** Galloway, Tom**;** Palmer, Wini V. Eakes, Wyatt**;** Moyer, Ben**;** Cooper, A.**;** Parker, Ralph**;** Freeman, R. S.

Row 12 Down: Legions, K.**;** Kirby, H. L.**;** Butler, Bob**;** Farar, Bill**;** Farrar, H. L.**;** McDonald, H.**;** Hamilton, H.**;** Allmon, E.**;** Lasley, Bruce**;** Coker, Wade

Row 13 Down: Pack, Marvin**;** Branson, Wayne**;** Flatt, Charles**;** Porch, Billie**;** Jackson, J. Kuykendall, L.**;** Carlton, D.**;** Hamilton, Con**;** Smith, V**;** Hall, Guy

Row 14 Down: Williams, J. E.**;** Fletcher, W.**;** Flatt, Vern**;** Cooper, W.**;** Wyatt, Ewing Kuykendall, H.**;** Edwards, Charles**;** Clark, Robert**;** Smith, Joe D.**;** Hall, James

INDEX

www.ingramcontent.com/pod-product-compliance
Lightning Source LLC
Chambersburg PA
CBHW041425090426

42741CB00002B/36